To Order Additional Copies

Available at
HolyCowConsulting.com/publications
AMAZON.COM

Publication Date: August 2016

_____

Bulk Orders:
russ@crowsfeetconsulting.com
614-208-4090
Discounts Available

Author Events Coordinator:
Shawn Kelly
shawnkelly.rn@gmail.com
614.216.5537

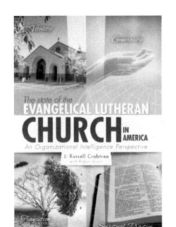

The State of the Evangelical Lutheran Church in America

An Organizational Intelligence Perspective
J. Russell Crabtree

$12.95 US • Paperback
ISBN 9780997768701
6 x 9 x 0.4 • 100 pages

MAGI Press

❝ *...a must-read for congregational leaders, synod staffs, and synod councils.* **❞**

Bishop Wayne N. Miller

The state of the
EVANGELICAL LUTHERAN
CHURCH IN AMERICA
An Organizational Intelligence Perspective

J. Russell Crabtree
with Robyn Strain

Published by Magi Press
ISBN: 978-0-9977687-0-1

WHAT CHURCH LEADERS ARE SAYING ABOUT
The State of the ELCA

When ELCA pastors are ordained, one of the promises we make in our ordination vows is to not offer illusory hope. Russ Crabtree helps us live out that vow in this small book. It provides a clear evidence-based approach to assessing where we are as a church. In New England, we now make use of the CAT (Congregational Assessment Tool) as the primary instrument for helping our congregation live in the present, and plan with honesty for the future.

BISHOP JAMES HAZELWOOD, NEW ENGLAND SYNOD

Once again, Russell Crabtree has challenged us with a call to base our planning and practice on evidence rather than preconceptions or anecdotal biases. This book is a must-read for congregational leaders, synod staffs, and synod councils. For those who have ears to hear it will guide us into more effective and faithful leadership.

BISHOP WAYNE N. MILLER, METROPOLITAN CHICAGO SYNOD

Author and motivational speaker Denis Waitley says, "There are two primary choices in life: to accept conditions as they exist or to accept the responsibility of changing them". For the pastor, congregation, and church leaders, to be agents of change, here is an evidence-based book that provides insights for meaningful ministry in the local church. From my experience in leading a transformational congregation, I found myself saying as I was reading, "Yes, this is most certainly true." Mining these pages for the nuggets of wisdom will raise the bar of dynamic ministry in your setting. The church depends on you—and so does Jesus.

REV. RON QUALLEY, ELCA PASTOR, FAIRFAX/CLIFTON, VA

All ELCA pastors and council leaders will find much in this groundbreaking book to stimulate thinking, and conversation. Russ Crabtree and the team of Holy Cow! Consulting provide evidence that has the potential for congregations to discover effective practices, refashioned priorities and renewed hope for the future. Our congregation has made use of the CAT (Congregational Assessment Tool) twice in the past five years and it's been transformational for our mission and a pastoral succession planning process. You owe it to yourself to read this book.

PASTOR KURT M. JACOBSON, ELCA PASTOR, EAU CLAIRE, WI

In a world where congregational systems are more and more complicated, resources are increasingly constricted, and culture is shifting sand under our feet, organizational intelligence for use in churches is like a beacon in a storm. Russ Crabtree's continued commitment to the banner of evidence based discernment, particularly in the context of the ELCA, offers honest analysis, hard truths, and hopeful options for a denomination willing to listen well and count the cost. This book is a gift to the Lutheran church.

MICHELLE SNYDER, EXECUTIVE DIRECTOR, PITTSBURGH PASTORAL INSTITUTE

The State of the ELCA captures in metrics how churches today need to be approaching the mid-21st Century. It's time to get past the fear of doing something different. This book has the data to support doing something different and points the direction in which today's churches need to go.

KELI RUGENSTEIN, CLERGY AND CONGREGATION CONSULTING, TROY, NY

*We shall not cease from exploration
And the end of all our exploring
Will be to arrive where we started
And know the place for the first time.*

These lines from a T. S. Eliot poem came to mind when I read the manuscript of the latest Russ Crabtree contribution to the discipline of organizational intelligence. From the vantage point of my service as the council president of four Lutheran congregations, the chief academic officer at three ELCA colleges, and a consultant for about forty ELCA congregations in the areas of pastoral succession, mission planning and stewardship ministry, I now see our church in new ways through Crabtree's sharp eyes. As a devotee of evidence-based discernment, I hope that pastors, leaders and members of the ELCA will not cease from exploring the meaning of Crabtree's findings and arrive where we know the church for the first time. Then we may truly become more effective agents of meaningful change and facilitators of enhanced congregational vitality.

DR. JAMES L. PENCE, WALKALONG CONSULTING

Dedicated to

Rev. Dr. Grayson L. Tucker, Jr.

1925-2013

Father of organizational intelligence in faith communities

The state of the
EVANGELICAL LUTHERAN
CHURCH IN AMERICA
An Organizational Intelligence Perspective

Contents

Acknowledgements

Nearly 60,000 Evangelical Lutheran Church in America (ELCA) Lutherans contributed to this book, both clergy and lay. The vast majority of these must remain unnamed because the contribution was an anonymous, though very personal, sharing of their thoughts through a series of questions they chose to answer. This makes it difficult to speak in any possessive way about the discoveries in this book. It is not so much what I have discovered, but what we have discovered together.

As the reader will learn in these pages, one of the messages members send is that their experience of the church is significantly impacted by whether they believe their voices are heard. This book is an earnest attempt to honor those voices by distilling what is most edifying to the church out of literally tens of thousands of pages.

However in the midst of a multitude too great to number, a few names are important to mention. I want to thank Emily Swanson, owner of Holy Cow! Consulting, not only for making available the database for this analysis but also for ably editing the text. Thanks also goes to Heather Clark for her terrific graphic design, inside and out, cover to cover.

It is always important to have the support of critical thinkers who will read early versions of a manuscript, make invaluable suggestions, and then take their place squarely in your corner. These precious folks include Dr. James Pence, Michelle Snyder, Rev. Tim Johnson, Rev. Rebecca McClain, and Rev. James Hanna.

I am also grateful for the collection of consultants that have begun to integrate organizational intelligence into their work. For this particular book, I am especially pleased for the formation of the Association of Evidence-Based Practitioners who have co-published this book with me.

Special thanks goes to Robyn Strain who conducted interviews with four pastors of transformational congregations and summarized those conversations in the content of the last two chapters of the book. Hats off to these pastors for being willing to share their learnings, a sharing that happens far too infrequently in the church.

As always, my wife Shawn, who offers unflagging support for all my writing and the crazy ways in which I do it, helped make this book possible in a hundred different ways, including proofreading early and late editions of the manuscript.

May 5, 2016

Preface

Dr. Grayson Tucker served as the Dean of Louisville Presbyterian Seminary for seven years. In the early 1970's, Dr. Tucker fell under the guidance and inspiration of Dr. Ron Lippitt, Professor Emeritus of Sociology and Psychology at the University of Michigan. Dr. Lippitt encouraged him to integrate the learnings of organizational research with the operations of the church. The research work of Dean Hoge, Professor of Sociology at the Catholic University of America, also provided impetus for a more intentional evaluation of congregational health. In 1974, Dr. Tucker created an assessment instrument for congregations which he named "The Church Planning Questionnaire."

Using this instrument, he began to help congregations with their planning processes. However, his vision went beyond that. After several years, Dr. Tucker had collected enough information from individual congregations that he could begin to aggregate the data in a way that allowed him to identify patterns of congregational health. From those patterns, he made some astonishing discoveries. For example, he found that the spiritual practices of members had almost no impact upon the overall health of congregations, but did correlate with financial giving. Historically, Dr. Tucker's methodology and findings have been largely ignored in the church.

After he retired in 1989, I continued his work doing little more than build upon his original vision. As a team began to form around evidence-based work, we developed a number of customizations to his instrument for applications such as strategic planning, pastoral transitions, and financial campaigns. We also developed similar instruments for church boards, church staffs, and middle judicatories.

Around 2010, I took his idea of aggregating data and turned it into an information management system for middle judicatories called inSight™. The concept was simple. inSight™ takes the annual reports generated by local congregations, adds the dimensions offered by Tucker's tool, and generates dashboards so that middle judicatory leaders could improve the way they resourced congregations and supported clergy.

This book represents the next stage in that vision: develop a large enough database so that patterns could be reliably discerned for congregations in an entire denominational family. I have begun with the Evangelical Lutheran Church in America, but subsequent books will be forthcoming for Presbyterians (PCUSA), Episcopalians, the United Church of Christ, and United Methodists.

As Dr. Tucker discovered back in the mid 1970's, I have learned that a great deal of resistance still exists in faith communities to any substantial use of organizational intelligence. In spite of the fact that major denominations have research functions at the national level, decision making is still mostly driven by impressions, anecdotes, and authority. However, a few courageous leaders are adopting evidence-based discernment processes and with good success. Their efforts are bearing fruit at both the congregation and middle judicatory levels.

The development of organizational intelligence has been a team effort, beginning with Dr. Tucker and his colleagues, but now expanding to include the leadership of Holy Cow! Consulting and a number of very capable practitioners. When I speak of the general methodology and discoveries of organizational intelligence I will use the plural "we" to include them. When I speak of the specific analysis referenced in this book, I will use the personal pronoun.

Several years before his death in 2013, I called Grayson Tucker on the phone to tell him how his original vision was being expanded and increasingly embraced across the church. He wept.

J. Russell Crabtree

April 23, 2016

Part I

Perspectives, Experiences, and Aspirations

Introduction to Part I

As stated in the title, this book explores the state of the Evangelical Lutheran Church in America with a focus on organizational intelligence. Organizational intelligence gives ear to the PEA's of members: perspectives, experiences, and aspirations.[1] Given that focus, I will not replicate data on membership, attendance, or giving that is readily available through the ELCA denominational offices, nor will I engage in an analysis of that data. Likewise, leaders generally do a thorough job of compiling lists of the ministries of ELCA congregations and synods in their annual reports. I will not replicate that work by listing those in this book.

The perspective from which members view their church or congregation is as substantive as the brick and mortal that gives them shelter from the elements. When Jesus returned to his home town, his neighbors' perspective that he was simply a carpenter gone rogue resulted in his doing *"no mighty work"* (Mark 6:5 KJV). The perspectives of members alternatively open or close down possibilities.

Churches and congregations are also centers of experience. While they engage in the formation of faith and harnessing collective purpose, it is the experience itself that is often instrumental in shaping both thought and behavior. It is worth noting that Martin Luther's religious conversion is referred to as his "Tower Experience" not his tower exegesis.[2] He speaks of it as words striking his conscience like lightening. Our experiences of the divine and our experiences of the divine mediated through the body of Christ are often inextricable.

Research indicates that individual attitudes and values do not reliably predict behavior.[3] This is particularly true in communities where members will experience a social penalty for enacting those values, or a reward for enacting contrary ones. Individuals with constructive communication skills and values may revert to indirect conversational patterns if they experience a community where direct communication is penalized. Individuals who hold theologically conservative perspectives may not reflect those in a community where more progressive views are in vogue.

Put simply, experience matters. This is especially true in today's cultural context which offers multiple options for personal and spiritual development.

Over recent years, yoga has become one of the fastest growing businesses in the United States with $27 billion in revenue and over 20 million practitioners. 91% of regular yoga practitioners are satisfied with the experience of their current yoga studio. Positive experience strengthens participation. It is difficult to not connect those two dots.

It would be easy to dismiss movements like yoga as simply feeding upon a consumer mentality in society. However the research suggests otherwise. 50% of yoga practitioners say they live green, eat sustainably, and donate time to their communities. Positive experience within an organization strengthens the impulse to reach beyond the organization. Again, it is difficult not to connect the dots.

The Gospel of Luke tells the story of ten lepers who came to Jesus seeking healing. The text says that *as they were going they were cleansed*" (Luke 17:14 NASB). I am interested in what is happening to Lutherans as they are going. I am not focused on developing a catalogue of Lutheran ministries but on the experience of members as they are going about those ministries. All congregations have worship ministries. I am focused on the exceptional things that are happening to members as they are going through those worship experiences.

288	57,000	801
ELCA CHURCHES IN THE UNITED STATES	PERSONS WHO ARE ATTENDING ELCA CHURCHES	LUTHERAN YOUTH UNDER 19 YEARS OF AGE

Not all experiences have the same overall impact on how folks feel about their congregation. Some experiences are pathways to a vital congregation; others are not. I will explore some of those pathways. Is simply being a Lutheran congregation a pathway to vitality? How about attracting members with financial resources? Or having a solid member retention strategy? We will look at all these questions and more to try to distinguish the pathways to vitality from the dead ends.

It is impossible to see from the outside how persons are experiencing their faith communities. However, it is possible to ask members to bear witness to those experiences. By analogy, it is not possible to see pain. However, you can get a good idea of a person's pain level by asking for an estimate on a scale of 1 to 10.

When we ask similar questions of Lutherans[4] we get insight into how they are experiencing their congregations. This is one of the larger studies of its kind on the experiences of members in ELCA churches encompassing thousands of members in hundreds of congregations.

Finally, organizational intelligence encompasses the aspirations of members as they contemplate the future. Aspirations have a corporate dimension that include, for example, priorities where members would like their congregations to invest additional energy. Aspirations also have an individual dimension, for example, how members see themselves involved in and supporting a pastoral transition.

The congregations included in this study participated for a wide variety of reasons: strategic planning, pastoral transitions, financial campaigns, to understand their organizational health, to track progress, or as part of an effort their particular synod has undertaken to become more evidence-based in their ministries to and with congregations. These congregations all administered the Congregation Assessment Tool™ (CAT).[5] I believe that our sample is broad enough to be representative of all ELCA congregations within a confidence interval of ±5%. (See "Limitations of This Study" at the end of Chapter Seven).

Our sample of 288 congregations includes every size, from smaller churches with under 100 in worship attendance to very large churches with over 1,000 persons in worship. While mega-churches and family sized churches possess

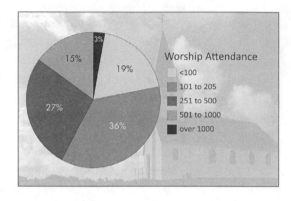

significantly different characteristics, they share this fact in common: member experience matters.

Because the Lutheran Church is a denominational system, it is appropriate to include in this study an assessment of the relationship between local church leaders (council members and clergy) and their synod. This book will also explore those perspectives, experiences, and aspirations using a separate instrument called Landscape.[6] Again, this is one of the larger studies of its kind in the Lutheran Church, and perhaps unique in its scope which encompasses both local congregations and synods.

In our work, we also realize that there may be cultural differences among congregations of the same denomination in different regions of the country. My analysis includes ELCA congregations and synods from East Coast to West Coast and everything in between.

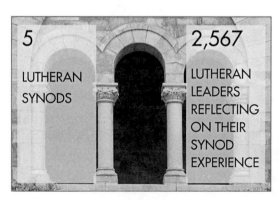

In Chapter One, I will explore how Lutherans are experiencing their congregations overall, and to what degree they are vital faith communities. It is important for the reader to realize that we are not determining whether a church is vital

United States

or not. We are simply reporting the experiences of members.

In Chapter Two, I will examine member beliefs and spiritual practices, including how beliefs impact experience. For example, how do member beliefs about the Bible impact their overall experience of the congregation?

In Chapter Three, I will look at the aspirations of members for their congregations, and the priorities that are important for their future. With the reader, we will discover how priorities shift for different age cohorts and why those shifts are important.

In Chapter Four, we will learn how members of Lutheran congregations anticipate and experience pastoral transitions - one of the most important periods in the life of any church. I will identify some missed opportunities and disadvantages of a one-size-fits-all approach to these transition periods.

In Chapter Five, I will deal with finances. My approach is not to look at dollars and cents, but to dig into the factors that influence member giving, and how Lutherans feel about annual stewardship appeals.

In Chapter Six, we will look at how leaders experience their synods, the factors that shape their perspectives, and the priorities those leaders have for the future.

Chapter Seven deals with the issue of discernment and the need to move from data to action through a grounded, prayerful, and creative process.

The numbers that pinpoint critical issues that congregations face are not complicated. Therefore, I primarily speak about percentages and have omitted references to means, correlations, crosstabs, percentile ranks, and factor analysis. Instead of tables of numbers, I have embedded a few important statistics in graphic images that I hope make for an easier read.

Several years ago, I heard a physical trainer give a talk.

"I am always asked, 'What's the best exercise?' and my answer is always the same: 'The one you will do!'"

The best book on organizational intelligence is the one you will read.

1 For a full description of organizational intelligence, see *Owl Sight: Evidence-Based Discernment and the Promise of Organizational Intelligence for Ministry, J. Russell Crabtree, (Magi Press 2012)*

2 *http://www.reformationtheology.com/2010/05/the_tower_experience_1.php*

3 *LaPiere, R.T. (1934). Attitudes v's actions. Social Forces, 13, 230-7*

4 *When I speak in this book of "Lutherans" I am referring specifically to members of the ELCA, not to other members of the Lutheran family such as Missouri synod, Wisconsin synod, or Lutheran Congregations in Mission for Christ.*

5 *https://holycowconsulting.com/get-started/churches/*

6 *https://holycowconsulting.com/get-started/regional-associations/*

Chapter 1

Vitality of ELCA Churches

VITALITY = SATISFACTION x ENERGY

As with any conversation, we begin in this study with more general questions and work our way to more specific ones. "How are you?" gives way to "How is the family?" and then to "How are things going with your boss?"

We begin our exploration with general questions focused on the two components of vitality: satisfaction and energy. The level of satisfaction gives us an idea of how members are experiencing the church overall. In over 25 years of using organizational intelligence, we have found that congregations where members indicate a high level of satisfaction are often church communities that reflect the Hebrew shalom, an expansive term that includes completeness, wholeness, health, peace, welfare, safety, soundness, tranquility, prosperity, perfectness, fullness, rest, harmony, and the absence of agitation or discord. Contrary to common belief, the research indicates that high satisfaction is never achieved by simply pandering to the self-interests of members. In actuality, shalom is created by a number of components that combine to produce a sense of wholeness.

57% OF LUTHERAN MEMBERS ARE CLEARLY SATISFIED WITH HOW THINGS ARE IN THEIR CHURCH

33% OF LUTHERAN MEMBERS GENERALLY AGREE THAT FOLKS ARE "GOING THROUGH THE MOTIONS"

While this level of satisfaction in a typical Lutheran congregation is problematic, it is significant to note that Lutheran congregations are not alone. In fact, in our data, Lutheran congregations fare somewhat better than a number of other denominational churches and have higher overall satisfaction and less polarization than Presbyterians (PCUSA), Episcopalians, and Methodists.

Nonetheless, simply being a Lutheran congregation is not a pathway to vitality. The "Lutheran brand" does not significantly predict the kinds of experiences that people are having in their churches.

Like satisfaction, we find that the experience of energy is a good overall indicator of how a congregation is doing. In its Latin and Greek roots, energy is nuanced in the direction of "work" or "force of engagement." This is the way we are using the word when we talk about congregational health and vitality. A high-energy congregation is one where members experience a compelling purpose or message combined with a high level of engagement, in contrast to a congregation where members are simply watching others or going through the motions of religious activity.

Then we need to examine the satisfaction and energy levels of three ethnic groups: Black or African American, White or Caucasian, and Latino. Of those three groups, Latino Lutherans are by far the most satisfied and

70%	**67%**	ONLY **58%**
OF LATINO LUTHERANS ARE CLEARLY SATISFIED WITH HOW THINGS ARE IN THEIR CHURCH	OF BLACK LUTHERANS ARE CLEARLY SATISFIED WITH HOW THINGS ARE IN THEIR CHURCH	OF WHITE LUTHERANS ARE CLEARLY SATISFIED WITH HOW THINGS ARE IN THEIR CHURCH

energized by their experience of the church, with Black Lutherans close behind.

Caucasian Lutherans indicate the lowest satisfaction and energy of any ethnic group. In fact, Caucasian males, arguably the most prosperous and privileged demographic group in the United States, are among the least satisfied. The least satisfied group of all is Lutheran households that make more than $300,000 a year. This suggests that simply increasing the presence of people with resources and power in a congregation is not a pathway to vitality.

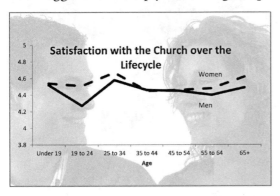

How Lutherans experience the vitality of their congregation varies depending upon their gender as well as each gender's age and stage of life. As teenagers, both males and females experience similar levels of satisfaction. That level drops slightly for women and significantly for males during the young adult years, but then rebounds rapidly for both through the childbirth years. It drops again and bottoms out for women in their 40's and then rises significantly as women age past 65. The bottom of this bowl represents an area of challenges for women, likely involving menopause, empty nest, and divorce. It is also where the highest suicide rates for women occur. The rise in satisfaction and participation may be a protective factor for women in their later years.

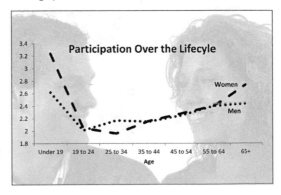

Men follow a somewhat different trajectory. The

dissatisfaction with the church takes a nosedive for males in their early 20's, another high risk demographic for which suicide is the 2nd leading cause of death. As with women, the satisfaction level recovers during childbearing years, drops slightly in the fifties and begins to recover around retirement age though not as quickly as for women.

The flat participation curve for men at retirement is happening at a time when the risk factors for males are increasing.

Internal and External Orientation

As with all faith communities, Lutherans experience their congregations in their two orientations, internal and external. In their internal orientation, congregations (a) care for the needs of their members and (b) change to meet the changing needs of members. In their external orientation, congregations (a) intentionally reach out to others and (b) adapt to meet the needs of those they want to reach.

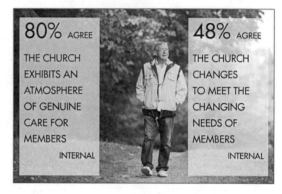

80% AGREE THE CHURCH EXHIBITS AN ATMOSPHERE OF GENUINE CARE FOR MEMBERS — INTERNAL

48% AGREE THE CHURCH CHANGES TO MEET THE CHANGING NEEDS OF MEMBERS — INTERNAL

Overall, Lutherans perceive that their church is more internally than externally focused, and have adopted the perspective that sharing faith stories is not a comfortable activity for most members.

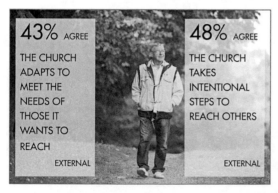

43% AGREE THE CHURCH ADAPTS TO MEET THE NEEDS OF THOSE IT WANTS TO REACH — EXTERNAL

48% AGREE THE CHURCH TAKES INTENTIONAL STEPS TO REACH OTHERS — EXTERNAL

Transformational Lutheran Congregations

In our exploration, we have identified two factors that are not pathways to becoming a vital Lutheran congregation: the

ONLY 17% OF LUTHERANS CLEARLY AGREE THAT MEMBERS ARE COMFORTABLE TELLING FAITH STORIES

Lutheran brand itself and attracting people with resources and power. We will discover other "dead ends" in later chapters. The good news is that there are Lutheran congregations that have much higher satisfaction and energy levels than the average congregation. I call these congregations transformational. Roughly 10% of Lutheran congregations fall into the transformational category. Nearly everyone in a transformational congregation experiences a sense of energy and enthusiasm. When we explore transformational Lutheran congregations and examine what they do differently, we discover pathways to vitality.

We notice in these pathways that they are not so much programs as they are a way of being or how members see themselves. Persons pouring coffee for folks during coffee hour can see themselves as simply pouring coffee or as offering a ministry of hospitality to which they are called. Either way, the activity is the same. The experience of that activity is quite different.

Transformational Lutheran congregations are a unique species among faith communities and exhibit many other qualities that are distinctive and even surprising. We will examine two of those qualities.

The group within typical Lutheran communities that experience the highest levels of satisfaction and energy are those who have recently joined. However, this level of satisfaction is gradually

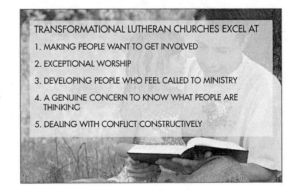

TRANSFORMATIONAL LUTHERAN CHURCHES EXCEL AT

1. MAKING PEOPLE WANT TO GET INVOLVED

2. EXCEPTIONAL WORSHIP

3. DEVELOPING PEOPLE WHO FEEL CALLED TO MINISTRY

4. A GENUINE CONCERN TO KNOW WHAT PEOPLE ARE THINKING

5. DEALING WITH CONFLICT CONSTRUCTIVELY

74% OF LUTHERANS WHO HAVE JOINED THE CHURCH IN THE LAST YEAR ARE CLEARLY SATISFIED WITH HOW THINGS ARE IN THEIR CHURCH.

10 YEARS AFTER JOINING ONLY **54%** OF LUTHERANS ARE CLEARLY SATISFIED WITH HOW THINGS ARE IN THEIR CHURCH.

eroded over time in the lives of those with longer tenure, bottoming out after about ten years. The lower morale of long time Lutheran members is offset by the higher morale of those new members joining the church. This suggests that recruiting and retaining new members is not a pathway to sustaining vitality in typical Lutheran congregations. Even if members stay involved, their satisfaction levels drop significantly over time resulting in lower morale and fewer strategic options.

Transformational Lutheran congregations exhibit a significantly different quality. Amazingly, not only do they begin with higher satisfaction, but even after 20 years, the satisfaction level has not significantly decreased. This means that new members in a transformational congregation do not go through a period of

85% OF LUTHERANS WHO HAVE JOINED THE CHURCH IN THE LAST YEAR ARE CLEARLY SATISFIED WITH HOW THINGS ARE IN THEIR CHURCH.

20 YEARS AFTER JOINING **84%** OF LUTHERANS ARE *STILL* SATISFIED WITH HOW THINGS ARE IN THEIR CHURCH.

disillusionment before they can "get into reality." It also suggests that new members are not required to balance out the lower morale of long tenured members.

There is a second characteristic that is distinctive and is significant for transformational Lutheran congregations. As we have seen, in a typical Lutheran church about 33% of members generally agree that there isn't much enthusiasm in the church and there is the experience of "going through the motions." One would expect that as members get more involved, a clearer sense of purpose would emerge. In fact, greater participation in a typical Lutheran congregation has a relatively small impact; a third of those more active members still perceive that the church is simply going through the motions.

In a transformational Lutheran congregation, a much smaller percentage of the members feel the church is going through the

IN A TYPICAL LUTHERAN CHURCH, INCREASED PARTICIPATION HAS LITTLE EFFECT ON THE **33%** WHO FEEL A LACK OF ENTHUSIASM

IN A TRANSFORMA-TIONAL LUTHERAN CHURCH, INCREASED PARTICIPATION CUTS A PERCEPTION OF MEANINGLESS MOTION IN HALF

motions. Equally significant is that as members move from non-participation to participation, the number of members who think there is little enthusiasm in the church drops in half. In other words, getting members more involved in a transformational Lutheran congregation is much more likely to have a sizable, positive impact upon member perceptions of purpose and energy in the church. Getting people more involved in a typical Lutheran congregation will have a relatively small effect. Increased participation is not a pathway to vitality for most Lutheran congregations.

Reinvention Congregations

On the other hand, there are a significant number of Lutheran churches that are facing difficulty, not simply due to a loss of members and money, but because their members are not experiencing their congregation as a community of shalom and purpose. We refer to these as reinvention

1 in 9

LUTHERAN CHURCHES HAVE SATISFACTION AND ENERGY SCORES SO LOW THAT THEY ARE IN NEED OF RE-INVENTION

congregations, that is, congregations that need to reinvent themselves.

29% OF MEMBERS IN REINVENTION LUTHERAN CHURCHES BELIEVE THE CHURCH MAKES WORSHIP CHANGES TO REACH THOSE IN THEIR COMMUNITY

There are several factors that characterize reinvention congregations. First, they tend to be internally focused. They are much more likely to make changes to meet the needs of their own members than they are to meet the needs of those they want to reach in the community.

63%	1 YEAR AFTER JOINING ONLY	10 YEARS AFTER JOINING ONLY
OF LUTHERANS WHO JOIN REINVENTION CHURCHES ARE CLEARLY SATISFIED WITH HOW THINGS ARE IN THEIR FIRST YEAR.	45% OF LUTHERANS IN REINVENTION CHURCHES ARE CLEARLY SATISFIED WITH HOW THINGS ARE IN THEIR CHURCH.	28% OF LUTHERANS IN REINVENTION CHURCHES ARE CLEARLY SATISFIED WITH HOW THINGS ARE IN THEIR CHURCH.

A second characteristic is revealed in how these congregations affect their new members over the duration of that membership. New members joining reinvention congregations have relatively high levels of satisfaction with the church when they join. However, that satisfaction drops sharply after the first year and continues to drop for 10 years. This decline, combined with the fact that increased participation in the life of the church has no impact on the 60% of reinvention members who believe the church is "going through the motions," does not bode well for the spiritual trajectory of new members joining reinvention churches. Simply put, retaining members in a reinvention congregation is not a pathway to renewal in congregation.

High conflict levels are also a signature characteristic of congregations in need of reinvention. Again we are not simply interested in member opinions about conflict; we want to determine how members are experiencing conflict, specifically the degree to which it is disturbing to them.

Dead Ends and Promising Pathways

In the words of Martin Luther's Small Catechism, *"What does this mean?"*

25%	10%	2%
OF LUTHERANS IN A REINVENTION CHURCH FEEL THERE IS A DISTURBING LEVEL OF CONFLICT.	OF LUTHERANS IN A TYPICAL CHURCH FEEL THERE IS A DISTURBING LEVEL OF CONFLICT.	OF LUTHERANS IN A TRANSFORMA-TIONAL CHURCH FEEL THERE IS A DISTURBING LEVEL OF CONFLICT.

The astute reader is beginning to recognize that these are not simply numbers or data on a page. They reveal patterns that serve as guideposts for leaders making decisions about how to proceed. Even dead end signs are gifts. They save us the time and effort of traveling miles down a road that goes nowhere.

Let's summarize some of those patterns.

- Simply relying on the Lutheran brand is a dead end for church vitality.

- Developing a congregation where members experience a sense of wholeness and peace combined with the excitement of a clear purpose is a promising pathway.

- Simply seeking influential people with financial resources is a dead end for church vitality.

- Developing a diverse congregation energized and unified by an exceptional worship experience is a promising pathway.

- Simply relying on new member recruitment and retention or simply increasing member participation is a dead end for church vitality.

- Developing a congregation where members sense their own call to ministry exercised in an environment where they have a voice is a promising pathway.

- Simply focusing on the internal needs of members and a reactionary approach to change is a dead end for church vitality.

- Developing a congregation that gives expression to its core values through a purposeful engagement with the external community is a promising pathway.

We could explore many other ways that the 57,000 members in our research project are experiencing their Lutheran congregations including their experiences of hospitality and care, governance, faith formation, readiness for ministry, worship, and music. We leave that for a future endeavor.

Next, we want to turn our attention to the beliefs and spiritual practices of Lutherans.

Chapter 2

Beliefs and Spiritual Practice of the ELCA Members

Churches are not only centers of experience. They are communities of faith with beliefs and ways that they practice those beliefs. In this chapter, I want to engage in a brief exploration of those beliefs and practices. I also want to look at the impact, or lack of impact, of these beliefs and spiritual practices on the way members experience the church.

The Scripture

In a study titled Lutheran Theology: How Lutherans Read the Bible, Dr. Jeremy Myers writes:

We often approach the Bible with inappropriate expectations. We expect scientific and historical facts or answers or proofs when those were never what the authors intended to provide. It is important to be honest about the expectations, prejudices and baggage we bring with us to the text.[7]

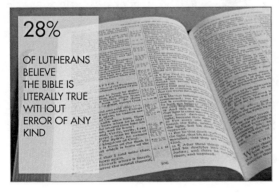

28%

OF LUTHERANS BELIEVE THE BIBLE IS LITERALLY TRUE WITHOUT ERROR OF ANY KIND

However, contrary to this statement by Dr. Myers, when we asked Lutherans if the Bible is free from error of any sort we find that a large number of them believe that it is. A slightly larger number of Lutherans disagree suggesting a significant diversity of views.

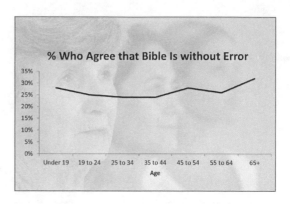

% Who Agree that Bible Is without Error

This belief in a literal Scripture that is without error of any kind is remarkably constant over the lifecycle of Lutherans. Even though many adults in their twenties are engaged in critical thinking regarding who they are and what they believe, we still find that one in four of these young adults agree that the Bible is without error. For older adults over 65, that number becomes one in three.

Conversion and Social Change

Another important belief focuses on the role of conversion in changing society. When conversion becomes the necessary first step in any societal change, it places a greater emphasis on the need to prioritize evangelism over advocacy.

34%

OF LUTHERANS BELIEVE THAT CONVERTING PEOPLE TO CHRIST IS THE FIRST STEP TOWARD A BETTER SOCIETY

A significant number of Lutherans clearly agree with the statement that conversion is a necessary first step. In fact, about 50% more Lutherans agree with this statement than disagree with it. However, in contrast to the belief regarding the inerrancy of the Bible, this conversion belief varies significantly over the lifecycle. More than twice as many Lutherans believe in conversion as the first step at age 65 as those in their twenties. This seems to indicate that as Lutherans age, conversion becomes a higher priority for church members.

Beliefs and Church Vitality

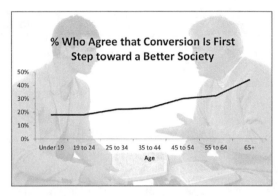

What is the impact of different beliefs on how members experience the vitality of their congregations? Very little, it would seem. The members of reinvention, typical, and transformational Lutheran congregations have relatively few differences in beliefs about the Bible or the importance of the role of conversion in effecting societal change.

Developing a particular theological perspective does not appear to be a pathway to renewal in Lutheran congregations. It is not so much what members believe that is critical. The differences among reinvention, typical, and transformational Lutheran congregations are largely a matter of how members live what they believe particularly in relationship to one another and the body of Christ.

27%	28%	33%
OF REINVENTION CHURCHES BELIEVE THE BIBLE IS LITERALLY TRUE WITHOUT ERROR OF ANY KIND	OF LUTHERANS IN TYPICAL CHURCHES BELIEVE THE BIBLE IS LITERALLY TRUE WITHOUT ERROR OF ANY KIND	OF TRANSFORMA- TIONAL CHURCHES BELIEVE THE BIBLE IS LITERALLY TRUE WITHOUT ERROR OF ANY KIND

Spiritual Practice

Before we leave this part of our exploration, we want to look at the spiritual practice of Lutherans in three areas: (a) the degree to which members connect faith to life, (b) the degree to which members experience the presence of God, and (c) the degree to which members engage in regular spiritual exercises.

While a majority of Lutherans work to connect faith to life, and an even larger majority of Lutherans experience the presence of God

69%	85%	29%
OF LUTHERANS ARE WORKING TO CONNECT THEIR FAITH TO ALL OTHER ASPECTS OF LIFE	OF LUTHERANS EXPERIENCE THE PRESENCE OF GOD IN THEIR LIVES	OF LUTHERANS FIND TIME FOR INDIVIDUAL SPIRITUAL GROWTH EVERYDAY

in their lives, these experiences do not find their source in daily spiritual practice. Less than a third find time for daily spiritual growth. This suggests that the spiritual connection for many Lutherans is experienced more through corporate activities, such as worship, rather than through a robust individual spiritual practice.

Once again, when I examine these responses across reinvention, typical, and transformational Lutheran congregations I find little difference. This suggests that neither the particular frequency of individual spiritual practice nor the cultivation of a particular religious experience is the pathway to a vital Lutheran congregation.

Dead Ends and Promising Pathways

What does this mean?

- Pastors may be surprised to discover the theological perspectives of their members. Depending upon the system, more conservative or more progressive perspectives of some members may be undisclosed.

- In our longitudinal research, the theological perspective of congregations is extremely stable. Changing the theological perspective of a congregation is a strategic goal that requires a 5 to 10 year time horizon.

- Theological diversity within a congregation is a non-factor in a congregation's vitality until it begins to generate conflict. However, once that conflict occurs, unmanaged theological conflict trumps all other vitality factors. Providing members with the skills to deal with theologically based conflict will not make a congregation vital but it will prevent conflict from spoiling one that is.

- Using organizational language, managing theological diversity is a hygiene function, like brushing your teeth. Simply brushing your teeth won't make people like you. However, never brushing your teeth will guarantee that they won't.

- Expecting either theological diversity or uniformity around a particular theological perspective to contribute to vitality is a dead end except as it finds expression in factors that do contribute to vitality, namely, offering exceptional worship, developing a sense of call to ministry among members, and honoring the voice of members in decision-making.

- The same is true of individual spiritual practice. Expecting a particular spiritual practice or its frequency to contribute to vitality is a dead end except as it finds expression in the factors that do contribute to vitality identified above.

This does not mean that either theology or spiritual practices are unimportant. However, it does require that we hold these endeavors to the high standard of actually making a positive difference. It was Jesus who set that standard. *"By their fruit you will recognize them."* (Matthew 7:16 NIV). Over teaching and under-training are dead ends. Promising pathways are found in making explicit the connections between belief and belonging.

As with the previous chapter, there is a much larger exploration of beliefs and spiritual practices that could be conducted in areas such as the importance of historic traditions, the role of the Bible in spiritual formation, the priority of faith commitments compared with other life goals, and the impact of spiritual experiences.

In the next chapter, we turn our attention to the priorities of Lutherans and their aspirations for the future.

http://www.elcayouthministrynetwork.wildapricot.org/Resources/Documents/Practice%20Discipleship/PD1%20Docs/Lutheran%20Theology.How%20Lutherans%20Read%20the%20Bible2.pdf

Chapter 3

Aspirations of
ELCA Members

Most church members imagine a future that is somewhat different from the present, and Lutherans are no exception. In order to get to that different future, additional energy needs to be invested in areas of the church's ministry that will steer the congregation in that direction. In this chapter we will be looking at those aspirations.

Missional Effectiveness

Since aspirations for the future mean little if a faith community is unable to turn those aspirations into reality, we begin by looking at how effective Lutheran congregations are at fulfilling their stated mission. A majority of members agree that the church is fulfilling the mission, and few in the church would clearly disagree, but a large number of folks are on the fence regarding that question.

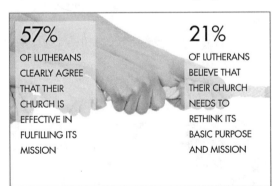

57%
OF LUTHERANS CLEARLY AGREE THAT THEIR CHURCH IS EFFECTIVE IN FULFILLING ITS MISSION

21%
OF LUTHERANS BELIEVE THAT THEIR CHURCH NEEDS TO RETHINK ITS BASIC PURPOSE AND MISSION

A significant minority of Lutherans clearly agree that the church needs to go back to the drawing board and rethink its basic purpose.

Future Priorities

When asked to prioritize a list of 17 goals, across all groups and sizes of church, Lutherans want their congregations to invest additional energy in church growth above all. Specifically, they want to reach

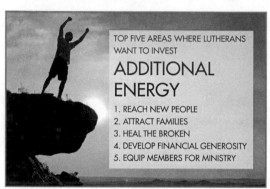

families with children and youth. This is true in nearly every community, including retirement communities, unless a congregation has been blessed with leaders who can appreciate a ministry to senior adults.

After church growth, Lutherans prioritize an investment of additional energy in healing people broken by life circumstances. The specific ways this brokenness finds expression depends upon the community - unemployment, addiction, mental illness, suicide, divorce, and spiritual emptiness to name a few.

It is easy for church leaders to invest energy in areas that are urgent rather than important. However, addressing urgent matters results in short term benefits that are rarely sustained in the long term. For every urgent matter addressed, two more emerge. Another name for the urgent is often "complaint."

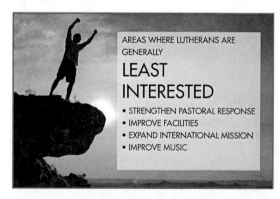

There are few areas which generate more complaints than failed expectations in pastoral care and music style. Yet, Lutherans regularly rank these near the bottom of the priority list for investing additional energy along with expanding international mission and improving facilities. Another way of stating this would be that changing the music in a typical Lutheran church requires roughly the same amount of effort involved in knocking out a wall!

Priorities and Generational Differences

What is important for leaders is that they understand the varied aspirations for different groups of people as they move through the life cycle. Many priorities remain the same for all ages, but some change markedly. Providing opportunities

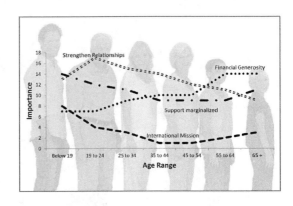

for developing and strengthening relationships is the top priority for young adults but a relatively low priority for senior adults whose relational networks are already in place. Developing financial generosity to support the church is a significant priority for senior adults, but is hardly on the radar screen for young adults. Young adults are much more focused on the external impact provided by supporting the marginalized and expanding international mission which is a lower priority for adults in the childbearing and childrearing years.

CULTIVATE GENEROSITY

Ambivalence toward Change

While Lutherans give high priority to investing additional energy in strategies that will attract new members, develop healing ministries, equip members, and cultivate generosity, a significant percentage do not generally believe that much change will be required to do so. This has the potential for putting Lutheran leaders into a double-bind.

If they make major changes required to meet goals, they may alienate a significant percentage of the congregation. If they do not make those changes, they will fail to meet the expectations of the very same members. This is made more acute by the fact that the church is now in a new place with the greatest breadth of generations in history.

58%

OF LUTHERANS INDICATE THEIR IMPACT IN THE WORLD IS LOWER OR MUCH LOWER THAN THEY WOULD LIKE IT TO BE

While most pastors of any experience understand this double-bind for the church, many lay persons do not. As a result, the church is set up to fail in realizing its aspirations. Managing change in the 21st century requires courageous leadership and adaptive followers.

Individual Aspirations

Individual members also have aspirations for their ministry in the world that go beyond their service to and through the church and congregations. In the response of over 10,000 Lutherans to a bank of questions from the Flow Module in the Congregation Assessment Tool (CAT)™, a great majority feel that their current level of engagement to impact the world as an expression of their Christian discipleship is lower or much lower than what they would like it to be, with only 4 in

ONLY 11%

OF LUTHERANS DEFINITELY EXPERIENCE THEIR WORK AS CHRISTIAN SERVICE

10 persons indicating it is at an appropriate level. This suggests that Lutherans have aspirations for their ministry in the world that exceed their current reality.

Part of the struggle of Lutherans is in finding a way to experience their work or vocation as an aspect of Christian ministry. While Lutheran theology emphasizes the importance of vocation in both lay and ordained ministry, 41% of Lutherans experience their work as only or mostly a way of making a living.

This suggests that one opportunity for congregations is to help members know how to reframe what they do in the world as ministry. The sense of failed aspirations combined with this lack of spiritual purpose in their work potentially erodes individual morale.

Backdoor Lutherans and Untapped Potential

One group of persons studied in our analysis consists of back door Lutherans. Back door Lutherans are those who indicate they are attending less than they were three years ago.

32%

OF BACKDOOR LUTHERANS CLEARLY AGREE THEY ARE SATISFIED WITH HOW TINGS ARE IN THE CHURCH

These folks represent a significant percentage of a typical Lutheran congregation (about 18%). If they continue on their current trajectory, they will likely become inactive and over several years can constitute a significant loss for congregations. Understanding their experiences and aspirations may be important.

In this analysis, I will only look at that population most at risk who indicate they are attending a third less than three years ago (about 4% of a typical Lutheran congregation).

There are a number of reasons that persons may become less involved in a faith community, including personal issues that have nothing to do with the ministry of the church. However, it is clear that back door Lutherans are less satisfied with the church than

ONLY 23%

OF BACKDOOR LUTHERANS BELIEVE THAT MUCH MORE ENERGY SHOULD BE INVESTED IN DEVELOPING GENEROSITY.

33%

OF BACKDOOR LUTHERANS BELIEVE THAT MUCH MORE ENERGY SHOULD BE INVESTED IN DEVELOPING RELATIONSHIPS.

members who are maintaining or increasing their attendance. They also tend to perceive an overall lack of enthusiasm for the church's ministries among members.

Backdoor Lutherans have roughly the same priorities for the church as those with no change in their attendance with two exceptions. They give a significantly higher priority to relationships and a significantly lower priority to developing generosity. Taken as a whole, this data suggests that internal issues are a significant factor in the decreasing attendance of many Lutherans. It also suggests the truth of the adage, "people join a church for many reasons, but they stay for relationships." The second exception regarding generosity seems to indicate that too much emphasis on the financial aspects of the church's ministry may accelerate the inactivity of backdoor members.

Taken together, this data seems to indicate that members have aspirations for both their congregations and their individual ministries that are not being adequately engaged.

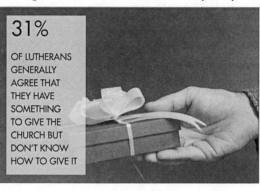

31%

OF LUTHERANS GENERALLY AGREE THAT THEY HAVE SOMETHING TO GIVE THE CHURCH BUT DON'T KNOW HOW TO GIVE IT

This is reinforced by the fact that almost a third of members indicate that they have something to give the church but don't know how to give it. Their invisibility to church leaders may lie in the fact that their aspirations do not lie in areas that are typical for recruitment.

Dead Ends and Promising Pathways

What does this mean?

- The nearly universal tendency of churches to prioritize reaching families with children and youth, even in communities with few families and large numbers of senior adults is a dead end.

- Providing opportunities for persons to establish and strengthen relationship with one another is a promising pathway for young adults in their 20's, particularly for those who are becoming less active, and men over 65. (See the chart in Chapter One, "Participation over the Lifecycle").

- Responding to and managing change is a promising pathway for vitality, particularly when both leaders and followers understand the importance of adaptability.

- Helping individual members understand and frame their work in the world as vocation is a promising pathway. So is equipping them as disciples to have the kind of impact in the world to which they aspire.

- Focusing all recruitment efforts on filling standard, fixed roles in the church's organizational structure is a dead end because it leaves many members underutilized. Building ministries around people's motivated abilities is a promising pathway because it optimizes engagement and reduces the number of persons who indicate they have something to give and don't know how to give it.

All congregations are dynamic systems that experience significant change from time to time, and Lutheran congregations are no different. In the next chapter I want to explore how Lutherans deal with one of the most significant changes they face: pastoral transitions.

Chapter 4

Pastoral Transitions in ELCA Churches

I t is said that in the absence of information, feelings become facts. There are few events in the life of a congregation that generate as many of these "feeling-facts" as a pastoral transition. The literature on pastoral transitions is awash in feeling words like loss, grief, anger, shock, guilt, depression, sadness, confusion, paralysis, and more. These feelings have become the facts of standard pastoral transition constructs.

There is no question that emotions play a critical role in how a particular pastoral transition unfolds. My position is not that these emotions should be denied, rather these emotions need to be bounded so that facts can also take their rightful place in a discernment process. The experience of loss in a pastoral transition is a feeling. The extent to which some members experience that loss, while others do not, is a fact.

In this chapter, we will explore how a typical Lutheran church responds to a pastoral transition. We will begin by looking at anticipatory data, that is, how members indicate they will respond to an imminent pastoral transition. We will also look at the diversity of member perspectives as they go through a pastoral transition. Then we will explore how Lutherans experience the church in transition under the leadership of an interim pastor.

ONLY **16%** OF LUTHERANS ARE CLEARLY UNCOMFORTABLE WITH THE TIMING OF THE PASTORAL TRANSITION THEIR CHURCH IS FACING

Loss and Paralysis?

We begin with the issue of loss. In any congregation at nearly any point in time, except immediately after a new pastor arrives, there will be some members who believe that it is time for a pastoral change and other members who do not. In a pastoral transition, the more folks believe it is time for a pastoral change, the less there will be the sense of loss at the time of a pastoral change.

In a typical Lutheran congregation facing an imminent pastoral change, almost half of the congregation clearly agrees that they are comfortable with the timing of the transition and that it is time for a change. The percent of members who are clearly uncomfortable is relatively small.

This suggests that intense feelings of loss are going to be experienced in a church during a pastoral transition, but not by everyone. While grief ministry is appropriate in the pastoral transition of a typical congregation, it should not be the dominant theme in most congregations.

It is sometimes assumed that the members of congregations experiencing a pastoral transition are paralyzed by feelings of loss and unable to make major decisions in the absence of a settled pastor. In fact, pastoral transitions become an occasion when members step up in their willingness to play a significant role in serving the church. Nearly a third of Lutherans facing a pastoral transition indicate they are willing to become more available to help congregations deal with transition tasks such as prayer,

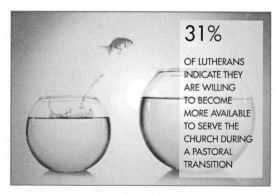

31% OF LUTHERANS INDICATE THEY ARE WILLING TO BECOME MORE AVAILABLE TO SERVE THE CHURCH DURING A PASTORAL TRANSITION

focus groups, committee work, celebration/goodbye teams, and welcoming teams.

Since participation breeds commitment, a wise church will find 30 significant transition tasks for every 100 adults who attend worship to keep folks engaged during the transition.

Financial Giving

In the face of a pastoral transition, leaders are understandably anxious about the impact on member giving. However, only about 3% of Lutherans indicate they plan to give less during a pastoral transition, and, in fact, a significant percentage indicates they plan to give more. This increase could mean a significant amount of revenue depending upon the size of the church and average family income.

13%

OF LUTHERANS INDICATE THEY ARE WILLING TO INCREASE THEIR LEVEL OF GIVING TO HELP SUPPORT A PASTORAL TRANSITION

For example, let's assume a congregation has 200 families with an average household income of $100,000. It is not unusual for 15% of the members of a Lutheran church to indicate a willingness to increase their giving to support a pastoral transition. If 30 households were willing to give an additional 1% of their income for one year, that would total $30,000. That additional revenue can be used for a number of purposes related to the search process such as travel, interview expenses and relocation costs.

ONLY 7%

OF LUTHERANS CLEARLY AGREE THAT THEY WILL EXPLORE OTHER CHURCHES DURING A PASTORAL TRANSITION

Exploring Other Churches

Previous research reported in my book *Transition Apparitions* indicated that churches with interim pastors lose about 12% in worship attendance a year during a pastoral transition. However, that is not how Lutherans anticipate they will respond at the beginning of a pastoral transition. A relatively small percentage of members clearly agree that they will explore other churches.

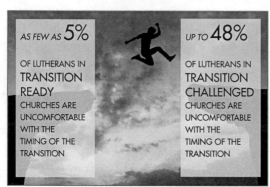

Nevertheless, about one in five Lutherans are on the fence on this question. This suggests that the degree to which attendance drops will largely depend upon what happens during the transition. If the anxiety generated during the transition is not appropriately handled, or if leaders adopt a boiler plate transition strategy that is not a good fit for the church, people on the fence may fall to the wrong side and end up "shopping" for another church.

Transition Ready and Transition Challenged Congregations

How easy it is to make a mistake using a one-size-fits-all approach becomes obvious when we look at the differences among congregations entering a pastoral transition. Congregations in transition can be as different from one another as a 3,000 member church is different from a 100 member church.

Some Lutheran congregations fall into a category we refer to as transition ready. Transition ready congregations generally exhibit the following characteristics:

• They are comfortable with the timing of the transition.

• They do not require a large amount of remedial work during the transition such as grief work or conflict resolution.

- They have a clear sense of their own identity apart from the previous pastor.

Other Lutheran congregations fall into a category we refer to as transition challenged. Transition challenged congregations look very different and generally exhibit the following characteristics:

- They are uncomfortable with the timing of the transition.

- They generally require a significant amount of grief work, and may have other remedial issues that need to be addressed as well such as trust in leadership or conflict management.

- Their identity is often focused on the pastor, either as an extension of the pastor's identity or in opposition to it.

In general, transition ready and transition challenged congregations require very different strategies and processes. Lutheran churches are no exception. Leaders in ELCA congregations may want to consider the importance of choosing strategies to match their circumstances at the beginning of their transition process.

Impact of an Interim Period

Once a Lutheran church is into a pastoral transition with an interim pastor who has been in place for six months or more, a mixed picture begins to emerge. Members are polarized in their perspective on how the church is really doing. When asked about the strength

32%	33%	34%
OF LUTHERANS IN A PASTORAL TRANSITION FEEL THE CHURCH IS WEAKER THAN IT WAS AT THE FORMER PASTOR'S RESIGNATION	OF LUTHERANS IN A PASTORAL TRANSITION FEEL THE CHURCH IS ABOUT THE SAME AS IT WAS AT THE FORMER PASTOR'S RESIGNATION	OF LUTHERANS IN A PASTORAL TRANSITION FEEL THE CHURCH IS STRONGER THAN IT WAS AT THE FORMER PASTOR'S RESIGNATION

of the church compared to how it was doing just prior to the resignation of the previous pastor equal numbers of persons believe the church is doing better or worse. This disagreement over how the church is actually doing has the

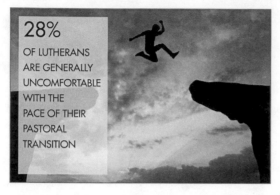

28%
OF LUTHERANS
ARE GENERALLY
UNCOMFORTABLE
WITH THE
PACE OF THEIR
PASTORAL
TRANSITION

effect of creating anxiety and even conflict. As a result, persons who were originally on the fence regarding whether they would explore other churches now begin to seriously consider that possibility. A congregation that was originally transition ready becomes transition challenged.

This mixed picture carries over into a number of other aspects of member experiences during a pastoral transition. Because members have significantly different perceptions of how their congregation is doing during the transition, it would make sense that members would also have different levels of comfort with the pace of the transition. Those who believe the congregation is getting weaker are going to want the transition process to move faster to staunch the loss of energy. Those who believe the congregation is getting stronger might be inclined to extend the transition process. This is precisely what we learn through our data from Lutheran congregations in transition.

It is also what we would expect when the same call process is applied in both transition ready and transition challenged congregations. Congregations that are transition ready would be frustrated by what they perceive as a glacial process that is weakening their church. Congregations that are transition challenged would experience the remedial work as helpful and strengthening.

As we saw earlier, about 31% of members indicate they will be more available to help with transition tasks. In actuality, Lutheran congregations receive relatively low scores from members for making good use of the congregation to help with the transition.

Finally, Lutherans are similar to other congregations during a pastoral transition in their tendency to under-communicate. Some Lutheran congregations set a gold standard for communication during a pastoral transition with over 80% believing that leaders are communicating well. However, in the typical Lutheran congregation, slightly more than half agree that the leaders are doing a good job communicating with the congregation.

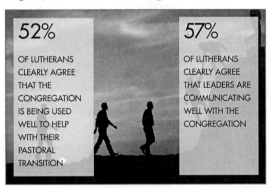

52%

OF LUTHERANS CLEARLY AGREE THAT THE CONGREGATION IS BEING USED WELL TO HELP WITH THEIR PASTORAL TRANSITION

57%

OF LUTHERANS CLEARLY AGREE THAT LEADERS ARE COMMUNICATING WELL WITH THE CONGREGATION

This contributes to a sense of confusion about how the church is doing and the unmanaged anxiety that leads to conflict and declines in participation.

Dead Ends and Promising Pathways

What does this mean?

- Lutheran congregations demonstrate a considerable amount of diversity in their readiness for a pastoral transition. Some congregations are transition ready; others are transition challenged.

- Applying a standard transition methodology to all Lutheran congregations in transition is a dead end. A promising pathway is the development of site specific transition plans.

- Lutheran members at the beginning of a transition indicate a willingness to support a pastoral transition with their time and money. Pastoral transitions that provide persons with a wide range of opportunities to make a contribution results in a stronger commitment to the end result, a new pastor on board with a congregation ready to follow.

- The experience of many Lutheran members indicates that opportunities during a pastoral transition are often missed.

In the next chapter, we will look at Lutheran attitudes toward financial giving.

Chapter 5

Financial Giving in ELCA Churches

The revenue stream for most churches consists largely of member contributions. There are exceptions. Some churches have developed significant endowments which are used to finance operations. A few own commodities, such as mineral rights, or rental properties which generate substantial revenue. In most cases, church leaders will need to cultivate and develop the generosity of their members to support the ministries of the church.

The Annual Appeal

Traditionally, this takes the form of an annual appeal during which leaders lay out a case for giving to their congregation who then respond, sometimes with a written pledge of dollars, sometimes with a more general pledge of support that includes other forms of giving (like time), sometimes with an implicit understanding of what members will give, for example, a tithe. Since leaders need to have some basis for planning and management, there is generally strong interest in some kind of annual commitment process on the part of members.

50%
OF LUTHERANS ARE CLEARLY IN FAVOR OF AN ANNUAL STEWARDSHIP APPEAL

7%
AREN'T

43%
ARE ON THE FENCE

While the support is rather tepid, Lutherans are generally in favor of an annual stewardship appeal. About half of Lutherans clearly agree that they are in favor of the annual appeal and only a small percentage clearly disagree. However, over a third is on the fence regarding the annual appeal. This suggests that leaders will generally need to invest a significant amount of energy every year "winning over the middle" and answering the concerns of the 7% who don't think there should be an annual appeal at all.

Interestingly enough, perspectives on the annual stewardship appeal do not vary much by different groups. Even young adults, who tend to give low priority to developing financial generosity, seem to have the same level of acceptance of the annual appeal as older adults who give it a relatively high priority. The small percentage of Lutherans who are clearly dissatisfied with the church still support the idea of annual campaign, though at a level that is somewhat less than the highly satisfied. The same can be said of those who are only marginally involved beyond worship. It is predictable that among Lutherans who are dissatisfied or less involved, annual stewardship campaigns will run up against opinions that the church is too focused on money about 10% of the time.

Future Giving

Many Lutherans envision a future generosity that is greater than the present. About one in four indicates that their total giving to the church in the next year will be more. Discovering what motivates giving is important if leaders are going to capitalize upon this impulse. When asked to rank five factors that influence their giving decisions, the members of a typical Lutheran church indicate that the most important factor in

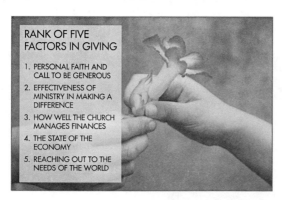

RANK OF FIVE FACTORS IN GIVING

1. PERSONAL FAITH AND CALL TO BE GENEROUS
2. EFFECTIVENESS OF MINISTRY IN MAKING A DIFFERENCE
3. HOW WELL THE CHURCH MANAGES FINANCES
4. THE STATE OF THE ECONOMY
5. REACHING OUT TO THE NEEDS OF THE WORLD

their giving decisions focus on personal faith and effectiveness of the church's ministry.

The general, and rather abstract, "reaching out to the needs of the world" is dead last as a motivating factor. However, this varies widely from one church to another.

Due Diligence and Mission-Impact Giving Systems

When contemplating giving, members of Lutheran congregations give higher priority to how the church is managing its money if trust has become an issue. I call these due diligence giving systems. Due diligence giving systems focus on the need for the leadership to manage financial resources in a way that protects them from misuse.

3%
PERCENT OF MEMBERS IN MISSION-IMPACT LUTHERAN CHURCHES SAY THE CHURCH'S MANAGEMENT OF MONEY IS THE MOST IMPORTANT FACTOR IN THEIR GIVING

23%
PERCENT OF MEMBERS IN DUE-DILIGENCE LUTHERAN CHURCHES SAY THE CHURCH'S MANAGEMENT OF MONEY IS THE MOST IMPORTANT FACTOR IN THEIR GIVING

In other Lutheran congregations, when contemplating giving, members give higher priority to the effectiveness of the church in making a difference. I call these mission-impact giving systems. These systems are generally comfortable with the way leaders are managing the church's resources; they are much more concerned with impact.

The percent of members in a due diligence giving system who indicate that management issues are the number one factor in their giving can be 8 times the percentage in a mission-impact system.

Other Giving Systems in Lutheran Churches

I observe several other types of giving systems in Lutheran churches. Here are two of them:

Contextual giving systems - In their giving decisions, members are more focused on concerns about the economy, compared to other churches, and how that might affect their ability to give. I tend to see contextual giving systems in communities hard hit by a recession or economic upheaval.

Dutiful giving systems – In their giving decisions, members are more likely to give out of the call to give regardless of the outcome. I tend to see dutiful giving systems among congregations that emphasize tithing as a Biblical imperative.

Motivations for giving also shift over the lifecycle. Younger cohorts are more motivated by reaching out to the needs of the world. A story-based approach will be more effective for them, connecting giving to the needs it can meet in the world. However, this motivation for giving typically declines over time and bottoms out in the child rearing years. Older cohorts are more motivated by the call to be generous and by assurance that resources are being well managed. For this group, a faith-based appeal combined with the demonstration of fiscal responsibility is likely to be more effective.

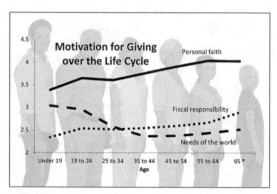

A site-specific, evidence based campaign will take these various factors into account when shaping the conversation with the congregation about their giving.

Dead Ends and Promising Pathways

What does this mean?

- Generating revenue for ministry will continue to require creative leadership in most Lutheran congregations.

- Developing messaging that is generationally specific is a promising pathway for developing generosity.

- Developing messaging that is site specific for particular giving systems (due diligence, mission-impact, contextual, dutiful) is a promising pathway for developing generosity.

I now want to turn our attention from Lutheran congregations to the larger system of which they are a part, their synods.

Chapter 6

ELCA Synods
and their Churches

In the ELCA, the role of synods is to unite the work of congregations within their areas, serve as regional support, and guide pastoral and other staff. As with congregations, our assessment does not attempt to catalogue all the ministries of the synods we studied, nor to replicate the statistical data on synods available through denominational offices. Instead, we are focused on the kinds of experiences that people have as they engage with or participate in the synod, the perspectives they have regarding the synod, and aspirations they hold for the future.

We chose to listen to persons directly involved with the work of the synod such as staff, synod councils, committee members, and rostered clergy, but also those in the role of making decisions regarding synod funding such as church council members.

We did not include members of congregations in the analysis because most congregation members do not have enough information or interaction with their synod to respond meaningfully to the questions.

The satisfaction level

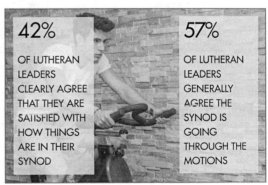

42% OF LUTHERAN LEADERS CLEARLY AGREE THAT THEY ARE SATISFIED WITH HOW THINGS ARE IN THEIR SYNOD

57% OF LUTHERAN LEADERS GENERALLY AGREE THE SYNOD IS GOING THROUGH THE MOTIONS

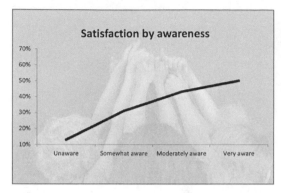

Satisfaction by awareness

70%
60%
50%
40%
30%
20%
10%

Unaware   Somewhat aware   Moderately aware   Very aware

of Lutheran leaders in the respective synods we studied is significantly lower than what we observed among members in their congregations. The good news is that there does not appear to be a significant degree of polarization in a typical synod as less than 10% of leaders are clearly dissatisfied. However, the percentage of leaders who generally agree that the synod is going through the motions is 33% higher than in congregations. It is difficult for any entity, profit, non-profit, or faith-based, to be sustainable in the long run when more than half of the persons who make decisions to provide funding are dissatisfied or on the fence with how it is doing and over half experience it as lacking purpose and energy.

In a recent publication by Kenneth Inskeep of the ELCA's Research and Evaluation office, he writes:

Much of the research suggests that members know very little about their synods or the church-wide organization. They experience their synod primarily during times of conflict and/or pastoral transition. Under both these circumstances, the synod can easily be perceived as an adversary… [n]othing is a substitute for pastoral leadership in every congregation, teaching and providing interpretation of the work of the whole church.[8]

The underlying assumption is that the primary issue that leaders and congregations have with their synods is one of interpretation and participation. At the denominational level, clergy are sometimes identified as a significant part of the problem due to their failure to adequately communicate the positive aspects of the wider church. But there is another reality. With only 41% of Lutheran clergy satisfied with their synod, the clergy satisfaction rate is no higher than that of lay leaders. Additionally, 48% of clergy generally agree that the synod is simply going through the motions. Given their direct experience, clergy are often in no better position to promote the work of the synod to those congregation members who are indirectly involved.

Increasing the level of awareness of the work of the synod does improve the level of satisfaction as does increasing the level of participation of the congregation in the work of the synod. However, while increasing awareness and participation is

helpful in improving its image, it only gets a synod so far. Even leaders who are "very aware" in congregations that are "highly engaged," satisfaction percentages begin to plateau around 50%.

Additionally, we see the same problem with tenure in synods that we saw with congregations. Satisfaction tends to drop as leaders are around longer. For leaders in their first year, satisfaction levels are at 48% but during the tenure period of 6-10 years those satisfaction rates drop to 39%.

A more substantial drop takes place with the age of the synod constituent. This could be because youth involvement with the synod is in relationally rich and morale building activities, like retreats, camps, and mission trips. It may also be a reflection of a natural process as the idealism of youth begins to wear off. Nonetheless, if synods do not find alternative pathways to vitality as leaders age, they will end up living vicariously through the enthusiasm of youth, and have less to offer them that is compelling in their later years. Given the limited contribution that awareness and participation can make to synod vitality, and the tendency for satisfaction to decrease with tenure and age, synods must do more than improve the interpretation of what they do.

Simply put, synods must not only change how they communicate what they do; they must change what they do. But, what must be changed?

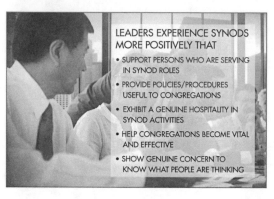

LEADERS EXPERIENCE SYNODS MORE POSITIVELY THAT

- SUPPORT PERSONS WHO ARE SERVING IN SYNOD ROLES
- PROVIDE POLICIES/PROCEDURES USEFUL TO CONGREGATIONS
- EXHIBIT A GENUINE HOSPITALITY IN SYNOD ACTIVITIES
- HELP CONGREGATIONS BECOME VITAL AND EFFECTIVE
- SHOW GENUINE CONCERN TO KNOW WHAT PEOPLE ARE THINKING

We get a clue from exploring where leaders focus in determining how they experience a synod overall. What makes the difference between a synod where leaders feel more satisfied and energized about the synod's work, and one where leaders feel less satisfied and energized? From that exploration, we discover that there are five key functions that contribute to a more positive regard for the synod. If we could wave a magic wand so that all leaders would suddenly regard the synod positively in these areas, it would be a different day for the ELCA.

A totally different approach to discovering what might increase the vitality of synods is to ask leaders where they would like their synod to invest more energy. In a list of sixteen possibilities, leaders gave priority to five, all of which focused on equipping and empowering congregations.

It is equally important to note where leaders do not want synods to invest additional energy. For example, leaders ranked "streamline the synod organizationally and administratively so that it makes better use of financial resources" dead last. In addition, they ranked "provide church leaders with the interpretive resources that will build more support for the work of the

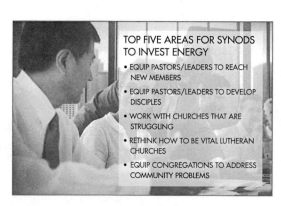

TOP FIVE AREAS FOR SYNODS TO INVEST ENERGY

- EQUIP PASTORS/LEADERS TO REACH NEW MEMBERS
- EQUIP PASTORS/LEADERS TO DEVELOP DISCIPLES
- WORK WITH CHURCHES THAT ARE STRUGGLING
- RETHINK HOW TO BE VITAL LUTHERAN CHURCHES
- EQUIP CONGREGATIONS TO ADDRESS COMMUNITY PROBLEMS

synod among members of the congregation," next to last. Contrary to the denominational theory that higher governing bodies simply need to do a better job "telling their story," this data set suggests that synods need to actually change the story by adopting a different set of priorities focused on developing vital congregations.

Dead Ends and Promising Pathways

What does this mean?

• Expecting clergy to do a better job promoting the work of ELCA synods is a dead end.

• Simply doing a better job interpreting or marketing the work of the synods to congregations is a dead end.

• Promising pathways for ELCA synods will require significant changes in how they understand themselves and the purpose of the work they do. Specifically, this will mean orienting their energy in the direction of developing vital congregations. This is already being achieved by a number of middle judicatories across the country.

---

8 http://download.elca.org/ELCA%20Resource%20Repository/context.pdf

Chapter 7

From Data
to Discernment

There are two major risks for the reader in dealing with the
information in this book. The first is that the data will not be
integrated into a discernment process. The second is that generalized
data alone will be utilized that is not site specific.

Risk #1: Lack of Integration

Data is not discernment.

That statement deserves to stand alone. What data makes possible is
an evidence-based discernment process which I defined in my book
Owl Sight.

   An evidence-based discernment is a process of discovery that
integrates organizational intelligence, core values, and an inspired
imagination to establish a course of action. The integration of these
three components produces a synergy through which each enriches
and empowers the other two. Individually and in isolation, each
becomes inert. We have all experienced instances of this synergy, and
when we do it leaves a lasting impression. We also have experienced
its absence.[9]

Data without Discernment

The failure to move from data to discernment finds two different
expressions. First, leaders can expect the data to make all the decisions
for them without paying attention to the core values of the Gospel.

No effective organization today can succeed if it throws its core commitments to the wind and reverts to a "give the people what they want" philosophy. I referred to yoga at the beginning of the book. Yoga doesn't succeed by inviting people to strike any pose they want. Neither should Christian leaders.

Similarly, in the absence of an inspiring vision the focus on data alone hollows out the collective soul. Creativity is required, that ability to combine disparate things and produce something that is both new and resonant with the DNA of a particular faith community. One of the sure signs that people have not yet thrown the creativity switch is when they ask me, "But what do we do with this information." My best answer: pray.

For example, when we see the drop in satisfaction for women in their middle years, what have we been missing? What creative steps might we take to deal with that? When we see the tepid rise in satisfaction for men at retirement, the very time when they are at increased risk for all kinds of problems, what creative steps might we take to engage them? I can quickly come up with a dozen ideas but that's not helpful if it supplants the creativity of local leaders and the subsequent energy and commitment that accrues to their own soul-deep participation.

Discernment without Data

The second expression of a failure to move from data to discernment occurs when leaders reject the reality presented by the data in favor of a pre-cognitive commitment. A pre-cognitive commitment is defined as the tendency to rely on common sense and opinions which are regarded erroneously as facts. Creativity becomes fantasy. My best example is that of leaders in a retirement community who nonetheless steadfastly commit themselves to strategies to reach families with youth and children! At higher levels of the church, I see the same pattern in leaders who steadfastly hold to the opinion that their primary problem is the need for better promotion of what they do when the evidence is clear that they need to change what they do.

Risk #2: Failure to Be Site-Specific

The second risk for the leader in dealing with the information in this book is the failure to be site-specific. Site-specific means "created, designed, or selected for a specific location." Discernment must be site-specific - Jesus was wrapped in swaddling clothes in Bethlehem, not taped into Pampers in Pittsburgh. Site-specific means collecting the kinds of information explored in this book for your particular faith community. Much of the data you have reviewed in these pages is averaged over 288 congregations to produce what we are calling a "typical Lutheran congregation." The typical Lutheran congregation does not exist!

We do fairly well in the Christian church in recognizing the value of certain kinds of diversity, but we fail miserably at honoring other kinds of diversity. Transition ready congregations are very different from transition challenged churches. Reinvention congregations are very different from transformation congregations. As a result, we apply one-size-fits-all solutions and wonder why they don't work. Or, instead, we simply ignore the fact that they are not working.

Lutheran congregations and synods must collect the organizational intelligence that applies to their specific communities and contexts. We now have ample evidence that this approach is effective at creating more vital congregations and middle judicatories. The Gospel the church proclaims and the Lord we serve requires no less of us.

LIMITATIONS OF THIS STUDY

This study was conducted by investigating aggregated data from churches and synods. Self-selection errors could result in non-representative samples from these various groups. The magnitude of this error for congregations is likely to be small given the geographic and size distribution of the population which is roughly representative of the universe of Lutheran congregations. Our confidence level in speaking of Lutheran congregations is fairly high.

Our ground is not as solid for synods given the smaller population

(5) of our sample. The data may be positively skewed for the entire sample given one synod's unusually high scores. However, the patterns we see in Lutheran synods are very similar to what we see in an extensive database of middle judicatories from other denominations. The degree of uncertainty on the data from synods is larger than on congregations, but not so large to avoid conversations about their implications.

The answer to concerns about validity, of course, is to expand the collection of data which we would welcome and for which we constantly advocate.

Robyn Strain now continues the writing with two chapters summarizing interviews with the pastors of four transformational churches, one large, one small, one more conservative and one more progressive. Remember, theological perspective is not a predictor of church vitality. Other factors are.

I end this book where I began with a statement from the introduction. If I have one piece of advice to pastors and middle judicatories it is this: use an evidence-based approach to identify, recognize, and learn from the transformational congregations in your region. Only one thing can prevent that from bearing fruit: EGO. Edging God Out.

---

9 Crabtree, J Russell. (2012). *Owl Sight: Evidence-Based Discernment and the Promise of Organizational Intelligence for Ministry (Mage Press, 2012)*

Part II
*Stories of Transformational
Lutheran Churches*

Introduction to Part II

I began the "Introduction to Part I" by talking about the organizational intelligence for a typical yoga studio. In this section I want to address this question: "What happens to Lutheran congregations when they exhibit satisfaction and energy levels approaching those of other effective enterprises in their communities which would include yoga studios but also public libraries and coffee shops?"

The answer is simple: *they become transformational.*

Transformational congregations have discovered ways to be vibrant and healthy in spite of national trends. They are characterized by corporate spiritual zest; encounter-driven, inspired worship; healthy, healing, meaningful relationships; purposeful activity in the world; a sense of being at the right place at the right time, both individually and corporately; and a nearly palpable atmosphere of well-being about the grounds.

Having worked in the field of organizational intelligence for over 25 years, I find it difficult for many folks to comprehend that when organizational intelligence indicates a church is transformational, it does indeed exhibit distinctive and remarkable qualities that are better experienced than described. I know this. I have boarded planes to fly to some of these churches and found them to be exactly what the data indicates.

In a variation of the Anna Karenina principle, unhappy congregations are unhappy in the same ways, vital congregations are vital in different ways. Just as a healthy person has many different options for how to spend a day, transformational congregations have many different options for how they can give expression to their mission. Yet, if you scratch below the surface, you will find many of the same attributes: vital worship, clear focus, genuine relationships, open representative governance, ministry that makes a difference, and priority given to serving the community and world rather than an internal focus on their own members.

The factors that make for transformation are independent of average worship attendance. Given the financial resources of larger congregations, it may strike one as counterintuitive to learn that larger congregations are no more likely to be transformational than any other size congregation. To illustrate this point, Robyn Strain interviewed the pastors of two transformational congregations, one small, and one large. A summary of these interviews can be found in Chapter Eight. At first glance, they look very different; upon closer examination they have more in common than not. Any congregation of any size can be transformational.

The factors that make for transformation are also independent of a particular theological perspective. In an age of polarization, of rally cries calling us to "get back to the Bible" coming from one side, and cries calling us to "get up to date" coming from the other, this also may be counter-intuitive. This is not to say that theological perspective is unimportant; it is. However, the factors that make the difference between a transformational congregation and one in need of reinvention lie elsewhere. These factors are discovered in the stories of transformational congregations of various theological perspectives as can be discovered in the summary of a more conservative and a more progressive congregation found in Chapter Nine.

I cannot stress enough that it is essential that pastors and middle judicatories use an evidence-based approach to identify, recognize, and learn from the transformational congregations in their regions.

Chapter 8

Interview of Pastors from Large and Small Transformational ELCA Churches

Resurrection Lutheran Church, *Channahon, Illinois*
Ben Ingelson, *Pastor*
Average Attendance : 70

Resurrection Lutheran Church in Channahon didn't begin as Resurrection; it IS a resurrection. Channahon and Minooka were rapidly growing communities in the late 1990's. Using the Pastor Developer model, the ELCA responded to the spiritual needs of these communities by starting a single church, New Creation, to serve both. The model incorporated significant financial support for the developing congregation, but within the first 6 years, the church had grown to the point of formally organizing. At this juncture, the ELCA no longer recognized the church as being "in development" and began to withdraw financial support.

Shortly afterward, momentum shifted and conflict began to arise around financial issues. Programs were scaled back or cancelled entirely and the church fell into a period of steep decline. "Camps" quickly coalesced and the ministry of the pastor was blamed by many for the failure of the church, further deepening the conflict. By 2008, the congregation faced two options: close the doors or restart the church.

The remaining congregation voted to start over, and Ben Ingelson began his tenure as the first pastor of this now very small congregation. The surviving congregation largely consisted of New Creation's founding members, most now in their mid to late 60's. Ben describes them as folks who had the "long view." Ben's voice still crackles with emotion as he talks about the ceremonial closing of New Creation and its resurrection.

On that last Sunday of New Creation's existence, they worshiped together, blessed the altar and physically left the building as one body, literally closing and locking the doors, deeply grieving over the loss. However, later that same day, they unbarred the doors and reentered as a new congregation. At the following congregational meeting, the new church was named Resurrection and the congregation latched onto the hope inherent in the symbolism of that name.

Understandably, there is a lot of anxiety around church closings. But, Ben says the actual restart was quite freeing. He describes his experience with his congregation as they faced what they feared the most: closing. Yet, there they still stood. Ben is quick to make the point that a part of the congregations' fear was allayed by the ELCA's willingness to come back in with substantial financial support. But he knew there were other urgencies. He told his congregation that "anything we can do now that will breathe life into this congregation, anything we can do to affirm that we have gifts for ministry right now, will go a long way."

Ben observed that there was a mindset and spirit of scarcity leading up to closing. During the final worship service, the reading from the Revised Common Lectionary was about the feeding of the 5,000. The timing of this really made an impression and the congregation began to shift from thinking in terms of "We ONLY have 2 fish and 5 loaves," to "Hey! We've GOT 2 fish and 5 loaves." They quickly changed their mission to include the words "sharing God's love" because the term "sharing" implies abundance.

They started living into this abundance. They decided to start doing things immediately with their small congregation, rather than wait for more people to show up. They restarted Sunday school. They developed a children's program even though there were no children because they knew they had to have the programs first to attract families with children. Much of what they did early on supported the ministries of other churches and non-profits. Their mantra was "We can live ministry right now!" Yet, they knew they needed something bigger, their own footprint, which would make this cultural shift take root.

As New Creation Lutheran Church, the congregation had purchased an adjacent piece of property with the intention of building. To the newly formed Resurrection Lutheran, the property was a glaring symbol of having fallen short. They began to think about the potential for that property apart from a new building. Over a period of 12 months, they developed a thriving community garden that provided fresh food to food pantries, connected people in the church with people in the community. The congregation had transformed something that had symbolized shortcoming and failure into something that symbolized creativity and adaptability.

Yet, it wasn't a straight shot to success. Even in the midst of the project, a lot of feelings of self-doubt kept creeping into their conversations. They often felt they were "not enough." However, they "just kept moving forward" and it became a victory for the congregation to pull off something that often seemed to be beyond their reach. Ben says that "one of the things I enjoy about being a pastor here is that there really is a spirit of 'let's try it, let's go for it, let's do ministry now!' There's a lot of permission here to try things."

This may be easier at Resurrection because there are no long established ministries or programs; at their core, they are risk takers. They just keep trying things despite the fact that, sometimes, they don't work. But, "we try not to lose too much sleep over it, try to learn from it, and try a different manifestation that gets at the same core values." They know that with growth, they will be able to do more, but they refuse to be a congregation lying in wait.

Much of the success of Resurrection is credited to the lay leadership.

The previous council was disbanded when the church closed. It restarted with no formal lay leadership and stayed that way for a full calendar year. This allowed former council members to step back and evaluate what they needed to do differently and how they needed to think differently. The focus was on how to live their mission of sharing God's love.

Part of the starting over model gives the pastor the final say, but they held many congregation meetings to strategize and plan. A formal board was not elected until 2013, and much of the governance structure is modeled after the teachings of Dan Hotchkiss in his book, Governance and Ministry. This structure essentially emphasizes the need for the board to focus on big picture issues, and avoid becoming mired in discord and minutia. The council also conducts an annual ministry and performance review of Ben's work and leadership.

Ben is aware of the need to empower leaders and broaden the leadership circle. He is working to move from an instigator of programs and ideas for ministry to an instigator of teams that are empowered and supported to make ministry happen. There is a "permissive culture" to experiment and explore, but he helps leaders think through different options, related to the mission of the church.

The current strategy for growing the church is to build relationships through outreach ministries, and they have had some early successes through a handful of leaders that make these things happen. The pastor is positioned as a resource and support, but the boundary is clear. If the ministries are to succeed, it will be the leaders, not the pastor, who ultimately make it happen. Ben's role is bringing the team together.

Leaders at Resurrection are reexamining existing ministries for alignment with the new mission. For example, New Creation, the former congregation, was known for garage sales. Previously, proceeds from the sale went to the general fund for the church; now they are returned to the community. The congregation is vigilant about balancing activities and programs so that they don't just support members, but, whenever possible, also support ministry opportunities in the community.

In short, the church has put a moratorium on any activity that reinforces the mindset that "we don't have enough." This abundance mentality continues in spite of the fact that they are no longer receiving grant support from the ELCA. The church is able to sustain itself in part because of growth, but people are also just more generous. For the first quarter of 2016, receipts were $40,000. For the same period in 2009, receipts totaled $15,000.

For this congregation, hospitality is a priority. It is common to hear folks speak in terms of "those who are members, and those who are not yet a part of our church." Because the church has not been around for very long, each person has a relatively recent experience of showing up for the first time. There is an understanding that if you are not a visitor, then you are a host. Each member of the church is called upon to make sure that newcomers are "welcomed well." The estimated return rate for first time visitors is 1 in 3, and the church has grown from 25 in worship in 2009 to 70 presently. Ben believes people pick up the genuine feel of community, but not in a limiting sense of "we're family," noting that sometimes that can make others feel like outsiders. Resurrection is a place where people who are curious about their faith are supported in what they are called to be and do.

Still, there are some struggles. They are working to figure out how to connect new people to current members. They have identified this as essential to their continued survival and growth. Ben worries about the impatience of the congregation to grow and do more, and he feels considerable pressure to always keep making great strides.

Finances can be stressful as well. Resources from the ELCA are dwindling, and the congregation has had to find ways to replace $40,000 in income. However, they are almost to the point of being able to support all the ministries they are running. Ben is concerned about the day in the future when he may feel called to serve another congregation and how that may impact the community. To a degree, he feels responsible for the survival of the church. But, he is working to shift the congregation's dependence on him to independence in leadership and ministry. He believes one key to this is the relational networks that are currently under construction.

As for the future, the congregation is clear that they have not done this work alone, and that they are uniquely positioned to pay it forward. They understand the fear inherent in the threat of closure and know how demoralizing it can be. But, they have identified and lived out critical components that have given them strength and courage to renew worship, develop programming, rebuild leadership, reach out to the community, and develop an identity that is grounded in a sense of abundance instead of scarcity.

The congregation is eager to share what they have learned. In fact, they see it as their responsibility. And this is exactly what truly transformational churches do. They are always reaching, always renewing, and always giving.

Trinity Lutheran Church, *Eau Claire, Wisconsin*
Kurt Jacobson, *Pastor*
Average Attendance: 753

Trinity Lutheran Church is in a community of about 75,000 people and is one of nine ELCA churches in the area. It was birthed out of another long standing congregation in 1954, and it grew rapidly in the post WWII Baby Boomer generation. In the first eight years, it went through three building projects. The congregation was founded largely by young parents so the leadership developed worship and programming that served families. This spirit of reaching families with children and youth has prevailed throughout its 62 year history.

The congregation has had a clear outward focus from the early days, supporting international missionaries in Africa and other countries. The Trinity pastoral leadership has historically been very conscious of the importance of this kind of outward thinking and has focused attention on mission that goes beyond the walls of the church and beyond the local community. The foundation for this type of ministry has been in place from the very beginning. Kurt Jacobson, Trinity's pastor of 28 years, believes this continuity of ministry has been a key contributing factor to the congregation's lasting vitality.

In his early years, Kurt recalls a phone conversation with a member who was very frustrated by the church's focus on mission. She believed the church should take care of its own first. As the associate at the time, Kurt said that conversation really clarified things for him. He recognized, perhaps for the first time, that this was not a congregation for everyone; some members did eventually leave. However, these kinds of incidents did not derail or discourage the razor sharp intention of most members in the church.

As a function of their health, Kurt says there is a kind of immune system that serves the church well whenever there is an individual that rises up in some adversarial way or attempts to attack the DNA of the church. He describes the immune system as really "kicking in" in situations like this when, as a result, advocates for an internal focus are just not able to gain any traction. Kurt likens these congregational experiences to open wounds around which the system forms a scab that pushes the infection out before it can fester.

In response to the changing cultural landscape of the United States in the mid-1990s, Kurt began working with a task force to explore options for expanding and enhancing the worship styles available at Trinity. During this period, the congregation was given opportunity for input in a variety of ways and they were kept well informed regarding progress and direction. Within 8 months, a new worship schedule was introduced that not only offered new options, but a renewed traditional service. Although there was some push back from a few members, they respected the attention to detail, insistence on quality, and depth of experience offered by the new formats.

For the first year, Kurt and the team were careful to protect what had been created to give the experiment time to take root, and take root it did. There were significant gains in worship attendance and membership, particularly among younger folks. The older members who may have personally preferred the prior traditional style saw this growth and recognized that the change had been good for the church overall. These changes turned out to be fruitful for people of all demographics and not a single person left the church as a result.

Kurt describes his staff as joyful, energetic and committed to high quality. They each function as coach and player, learning from each other and sharing in one another's successes. His staffing model emphasizes the importance of having staff members in roles that fit their gifts and that give them opportunities to do what they do best, in work that is meaningful. Trinity has evaluated the effectiveness of this approach and discovered that every member on staff feels a sense of calling and purpose to the work that they do. Kurt believes this is an important part of the cohesion of the staff.

The council is a large body of 18 persons who are primarily involved in issues of policy and visioning. Kurt works with the executive committee to address day-to-day management issues. He explains, "Leadership is doing the right things and management is doing things right. The council's leadership task is to ensure that the congregation is working alongside the staff to do the right things in its mission and carry out its ministries for the sake of extending the kingdom of God."

Two years ago, the congregation overwhelmingly approved a motion to affiliate with Reconciling Works, an association of Lutheran organizations committed to a public welcome of the LGBT (Lesbian, Gay, Bisexual and Transgender) community. However, this initial decision did not include a provision to permit pastors to bless same-sex unions. A few months later, the state of Wisconsin provided for the legal marriage of same-gender couples. As a result, the Council has spent much of last year discussing policy issues regarding same-gender marriage.

Like other issues, these deliberations were not made in a vacuum. The Council solicited conversations with and input from the congregation. Kurt says, "This is a thoughtful, strategic group that knows how to wrestle with difficult issues, manage inevitable conflict, and they take leadership seriously by generously giving of their time, experience and expertise." His approach with them is to respond to questions with questions that stimulate deeper thought, and then he encourages them to confidently make the decisions they are called to make.

Kurt is retiring in July of 2016 and has given considerable thought to what it will take to sustain the vitality of the church into the future. First, he knows that it will be critical to maintain the external focus in ministry and he is hopeful that his successor will continue to nurture this pathway. Second, the church will need to continue to address shifts in the way people think about financially supporting the work of the church. Like many churches, members of older generations tend to be the largest financial stewards; one of the challenges for Trinity is motivating Gen-Xers to take on more financial responsibility. Kurt has identified a third element as well for Trinity's future: the level and quality of communication. He hopes it will continue to be a place of trust, where no secrets are kept, all questions are valid, and leaders are genuinely interested in sharing what is going on in the life of the church.

Kurt indicates that Trinity's greatest vulnerability will be choosing a new lead pastor who is a good fit for the congregation. He believes it will be incumbent on the next pastor to recognize the importance of Trinity's core values: building relationships, nurturing the liveliness of the congregation, and learning about and honoring the long standing cultural DNA that drives the mission and ministry.

If he were to stay another 5 to 10 years, Kurt would propose collaboration with other ELCA congregations in the area, all of which have seen decline in recent years. He would lead an exploration into the question "How might we be more effective in extending the kingdom of God in this community through working together in ways which we've never attempted?"

For example, there is an ELCA community on the campus of the University of Wisconsin Eau Claire. He envisions leveraging the experience and resources that Trinity can offer to help this congregation reach greater levels of vitality and effective ministry to students and faculty. He would even go as far as considering a collaborative staffing model that would support the university campus. He would also initiate the development of a daycare at Trinity and expand their food pantry, which currently serves 700-800 families a month from a small room.

Kurt is confident that Trinity's leaders and members have the know-how and resources to do those things and do them well. His goal in this work would be to continue to explore ways in which members can engage with people from different walks of life. Ultimately, he wants leaders and the congregation to ask themselves: "What is the next BIG thing God is calling us to do?"

Chapter 9

Interview of Pastors from More Conservative and More Progressive Transformational ELCA Churches

Christ Lutheran Church, *Hot Springs Village, AK*
Warren Freiheit, *Pastor*
More Theologically Conservative

Christ Lutheran Church will be celebrating its 40th anniversary this year, and as a vital ELCA congregation, it attracts retired folks from all over the country. However, the church has not been without significant hardship in its short life. In the late 1990's, the Council leadership was embroiled in conflict with many in the congregation. As a result of the conflict, the Bishop's Office of the Synod was called in. But, rather than put the church on administrative oversight as often happens, the Council was dismissed. Those council members left the church and a significant number followed. This experience left a deep and abiding scar, and Pastor Warren Freiheit recalls the fragile and cautious congregation he encountered when he arrived five years ago.

The church has struggled through other conflicts as well. There were notable differences over the formation of a mission church. Christ Church strongly disagreed with the ELCA's 2009 decisions regarding human sexuality, and some members left and withdrew their financial support. Nonetheless, the remaining members were committed to renewing the church and have had to take some relational risks to regain the momentum needed for effective ministry.

The congregation was aware that recovering from conflict is no simple thing, and that it takes much more than good intentions. It requires intentional ministry. With this intention in mind, the congregation created the Mutual Ministry Team (MMT), which plays a significant role in the life and leadership of the church. Members and pastor alike are confident in the abilities of MMT and their work enables the Council to focus on bigger issues facing the church.

Warren describes this as a very healthy approach. Typically, MMT members are selected based on their skills in deescalating a situation and their capacity in identifying the issue beneath the emotion. By the time an issue is presented to Council, it is clearly defined and can be resolved without the Council becoming mired in the attendant anger that is often a part of the initial presentation. The result is that concerns are addressed productively and members' concerns are heard. This is particularly important given the church's history of conflict.

Given that this is a well-educated congregation, there is a deep well of capable leadership. Warren has discovered that coordinating leadership in the church is critical to its success so that all have the opportunity to serve in meaningful ways while avoiding the risk of too many people at the helm attempting to guide the ship.

Inherently strong leaders also have strong opinions, and that is the case at Christ Church. However, they avoid divisive conflict because they value their relationships more than defending a particular position. They nurture and protect the quality of their shared life by abandoning self-interests and adopting shared interests. To this end, the church focuses its work on opportunities that simultaneously fit members' gifts, give them the opportunity to serve the community well and build deep connections among members.

Like other retirement communities, Christ Church faces unique challenges in maintaining membership. Some members are lost to death each year, while others move back home to be with family. It is tempting in such circumstances to shift the focus of the church to reaching families with children and youth. However, Christ Church has deliberated and discerned that its calling is to be present to the retired persons in the community around them. In other words, they choose to play to their strengths: formation ministries that nurture genuine spirituality, and clear focus on mission to and through retirees.

Warren identifies the connection of the work of the church to the mission as critical to its future strength. When he first arrived at Christ Church, most members were of the Builder Generation, typically very dedicated individuals who deeply value loyalty. Supporting the work of their church is part of their DNA.

Based on his experiences in other churches around the country, Warren is concerned that younger generations may operate from a different set of values that will not necessarily translate into the commitment to the church he sees in Christ Church's current members. Younger folks also tend to travel extensively and are simply not present many weeks out of the year. He senses that it will be up to the Builders to share their passion and experiences in palpable ways so that those younger than themselves will pick up the torch.

However, the capacity for outreach is only made possible by the sense of shalom experienced by members within. This is a congregation that values relationship above all else. In the past, they had seen those relationships compromised and severed by conflict. For a congregation like Christ Church, there is no ministry outside of relationship. Perhaps they knew this instinctively because they committed themselves to intentional ministry that built trust and a pathway through conflict before it became divisive again.

First Lutheran Church, *Waltham, MA*
Tom Maehl, *Pastor*
More Theologically Progressive

First Lutheran Church was founded in 1889. When Tom Maehl began his pastorate in 1999, the congregation was coming through a period of conflict and division. There was also fear that it would be unable to sustain itself beyond an endowment that would dry up in 18 months. The church was about half its current size and comprised primarily of folks 65 years of age and older.

In spite of all of that, Tom encountered a congregation committed to making things work. The leadership was open, adaptive, willing to try new things, and eager to share leadership with others. Since that time, worship attendance has doubled and the congregation has become more multi-generational. Offering receipts have gone from $60,000 in 1999 to $220,000 in 2015.

First Lutheran is now a professionally transient population. Many people have moved to the community for graduate school or high tech jobs in the Boston area. Some stay, but others are transferred or take work elsewhere in the country and move away. Tom estimates that of the 150 new members in the last 16 years, roughly half of them have moved on. As a result, cohesion in ministry and leadership is a challenge.

On the other hand, at First Lutheran, ministry and leadership are always fresh. Tom has learned that it is important to be flexible, use the gifts of the people there at any given time, and work hard to cultivate meaningful relationships. He also recognizes the professional demands on many of the members and makes good use of their time by inviting them into leadership and ministry opportunities that are a good fit for the individual.

Three years ago, the church underwent a re-visioning process to create a mission statement they could actually live: "We perceive Christ calling us to walk together in God's love, nurturing faith, doing justice, and serving all."

Education and formation is an important part of this. The church hosts a large Vacation Bible School, conducts three retreats every year, and offers a variety of eclectic Sunday school adult forums. There is also a newly formed Justice and Service team that is experimenting with different and interesting ways of doing ministry. For example, they have taken the idea of the "flash mob" into ministry. They assemble as many people as possible for a brief period of time to accomplish a very specific task.

One Sunday a month, instead of coffee hour, the whole congregation comes together after worship for about 15 minutes and accomplishes something together. They have put together cold weather kits for the homeless, written to and prayed for every church in Flint, Michigan, written to women and children in detention on the border, packed lunches for local feeding programs, and packed kits for Lutheran World Relief. They call them "Flash Events" because there is no notice as to when they are going to happen. So the congregation experiences this sense of anticipation for the next opportunity. Tom finds these hands on activities particularly important for young adults who really crave opportunities to make a difference. He too is driven to make a difference and is very conscious of the assets and limitations he brings to his ministry.

Tom was not ordained until the age of 37 and believed early on that he would be called to serve just one congregation. Though he concedes that the Spirit may have other plans, he is proceeding as if his life's work is right here. If he is to serve one congregation for 30 years, give or take, he does worry about stagnating, so he is always trying to grow, change, and reinvent himself.

He thinks of his ministry as being divided into four phases. The first phase was about healing a broken congregation and making ministry relevant. He spent an enormous amount of time helping people reconnect with one another and mending relationships. At the same time, he began experimenting with ministry opportunities for younger members to make ministry more resonant with them.

The second phase was about stabilizing the finances and

infrastructure of the church. Worship attendance was growing which made survival less of an anxiety so people had more confidence looking into the future. They ran a capital campaign and repaired everything that hadn't been repaired in thirty years and balanced the budget. He identifies this first half of his ministry as being clergy-driven. In other words, he generated the ideas and made sure things happened.

Currently, Tom is in the third phase of ministry and is working to make the shift from the church's direction being steered by clergy to being steered by lay leaders. An example of this is a young woman who joined the congregation and wanted to continue some of the work she had been doing previously in El Salvador for Habitat for Humanity. Tom agreed to support her if she would lead it, so she organized the trip. He knew instinctively that he should not go on the trip. It would be important for the church to see that big things could happen without the direct involvement of the pastor.

He believes the fourth or last phase of his ministry will be about nurturing in the congregation an even greater independence in ministry. The key to this success will be continuing to build the deep sense of shared community and increasing the church's commitment to giving itself away.

Tom talks to the congregation about three relationships: relationship with God, relationship with others, and relationship with one's complicated and sometimes broken inner self. He believes his work as a pastor is to help people move more deeply into these relationships. Part of this ministry to his congregation is supporting members where they are. He recognizes that people are at different places in their lives that either create barriers or opportunities for growth. His work is to help people break through the barriers and embrace the opportunities, but in their own time.

Like most pastors, Tom is anxious about the future. On the one hand, he feels that the church is vulnerable. On the other hand, he knows that members are very flexible and able to adapt to whatever the future might bring. As he ages, he is concerned that he will no longer be able to connect to younger people. He describes himself as the ideal pastor for 1973 and worries about having the gifts to do ministry in 2016.

For this reason, he continues to expose himself to new ideas and ways of being a pastor. He admires the evangelism of a young colleague who boldly invites people to church wherever he goes. Recognizing the need to increase his own evangelism in the community, he begins to think, "OK, what am I inviting them into?" So part of his current work is getting clearer about how the church can better connect with the immediate community and how to better communicate what the church has to offer.

Tom knows that if they do not continue to do mission, "God will just walk down the street and go somewhere else, and we'll be the church that closes." He says that the "church must be agile, dynamic, and responsive. It needs to be a place that helps people connect their faith to daily life." Tom feels that he can be most effective if his primary work is helping people deepen their relationship with God, with one another, and themselves. "In this way, God has more to work with. And I guess I just want to give God as much to work with as I can. And then it's up to God."

What Does This Mean?

Returning back to the Lukan reference in the Introduction, we can now move beyond simply counting the number of lepers who came to Jesus, and also get a snapshot of the kinds of experiences they were having as they were going. It is difficult to deny that their "corporate" healing was an important part of that story. Whether members are being healed, inspired, energized, and reconciled as they are going about the work of Jesus is equally important today.

The Christian Church is nearly 2,000 years old. In the sixteenth century, Martin Luther capitalized upon a new technology that revolutionized its ability to communicate the Scripture to its members: the printing press. Roughly 500 years later another technology has closed the loop by revolutionizing the ability for members to communicate with the church: internet technology. Members now have the ability to communicate their perspectives, experiences, and aspirations to a degree that has never existed before on the stage of history. I have named this "Organizational Intelligence."

In one sense, the Internet is like the discovery of the printing press, only it's very different. The printing press gave us access to recorded knowledge. The Internet gives us access, not just to knowledge, but to the intelligence contained in people's crania...[10] - Don Tapscott

There are those who have been uncomfortable with the implications of both technologies. Historically, some have viewed the printing press as magnifying the subversion and destructiveness of erroneous ideas, resulting in multiple occasions of burning both books and presses. However, with regard to internet technology, it is impossible to burn down "the cloud." Passivity is the only option for resistance.

Fortunately, many of the theological grandchildren of Martin Luther are embracing organizational intelligence as the legitimate technological cousin of the printing press. If the proclamation of the Gospel by the church is the means of grace, they believe that the enterprise of understanding how members are experiencing that grace (or not) is a legitimate theological enterprise.

As a practical expression of that grace, organizational intelligence opens up a number of possibilities for the ELCA:

The Church can now identify its transformational congregations of all sizes and theological perspectives, independent of political and ideological biases. This opens up opportunities for celebration, learning best practices, and a contagion of renewal.

The Church can also identify dead ends and promising pathways for transformation. This has the benefit of shattering illusions, however deeply held, as well as opening up possibilities that may be unexplored or even counter-intuitive.

Through an intentional listening process made possible by organizational intelligence, the Church can identify faith communities in the early stages of decline rather than waiting for a crisis that requires a soul-bruising intervention.

The Church can now offer site-specific resourcing rather than generic or ideologically driven approaches. This opens up the possibility of:

- Pastoral calls characterized by a better fit between pastor and congregations, transitions that are more effective in setting the stage for the next pastor, and start up plans that result in fewer surprises and tripped land mines.

- Financial campaigns that are more resonant with the motivating factors of local faith communities and are generationally messaged.

- Strategic plans that optimize the specific assets of faith communities, shore up critical weaknesses, and capitalize on local opportunities.

Local faith communities can now take responsibility for their own destinies, make difficult choices to develop adaptive organizational cultures or embrace more familiar patterns, even if those patterns lead to numeric decline or closing.

Organizational intelligence not only offers the promise of more vital and growing congregations, but also saving hundreds of thousands of dollars in misspent staff time and psychological services for clergy who are suffering from the avoidable trauma of poor pastoral transitions and fit, as well as the damage caused by expectations made unrealistic by a particular context. The story of Sisyphus comes to mind.

I close with the words of Rebecca MacKinnon:

Would the Protestant Reformation have happened without the printing press? Would the American Revolution have happened without pamphlets? Probably not. But neither printing presses nor pamphlets were the heroes of reform and revolution.[11]

Organizational intelligence will not reform and renew the church. We still need heroes.

---

10 *http://www.brainyquote.com/quotes/keywords/printing_press.html*

11 *http://www.brainyquote.com/quotes/keywords/printing_press.html*

Association of Evidence-Based Practitioners
Appendix A

Holy Cow! Consulting
PO Box 304
Westerville, Ohio 43086
Contact: Emily Swanson
Phone: (614) 395-6326
Email: emily@holycowconsulting.com
Website: www.holycowconsulting.com

Des Moines Pastoral Counseling Center
8553 Urbandale Avenue
Urbandale, IA 50322
Contact: Diane McClanahan, M.Div.
Phone: 515-274-4006
Email: dmcclanahan@dmpcc.org
Website: www.dmpcc.org/consulting

Keli Rugenstein, PhD
Clergy and Congregation Consulting
Troy, NY 12180
Phone: 518-210-2486
Email: kelir@nycap.rr.com

Michelle Snyder, M.Div., LCSW
3524 Washington Pike
Pittsburgh, PA 15017
Phone: (814) 758-2056
Email: michelle.hanna.snyder@gmail.com

Samaritan Interfaith Center for Congregations
1819 Bay Scott Circle
Suite 109
Naperville, IL 60540
Contact: Nancy Sayer
Phone: (630) 909-9585
E-Mail: nsayer@samaritancenter.org
Website: www.samaritancfc.org

Walkalong Consulting, LLC
1210 Broadway St.
Suite 240 PMB 113
Alexandria, MN 56308
Contact: James L. Pence, PhD
Phone: (253) 219-3795
Email: jim@jimpenceonline.com
Website: http://walkalongconsulting.jimdo.com

About the Authors

J. Russell Crabtree is an Ohio native and graduate of the Ohio State University with a degree in engineering physics. He worked in research at the Eastman Kodak Company for three years in the area of optics and electrostatic control systems. He left industry to attend seminary and served as a pastor for twenty years. In 1998, Russ founded and served for five years as the executive director of Montaña de Luz, a project providing hospice care for abandoned children with HIV-AIDS in Honduras. In the wake of Hurricane Mitch he founded and directed Ohio Hurricane Relief for Central America. He was the co-founder and president of Holy Cow! Consulting which provides strategic planning, training, and organizational assessment. He also founded and currently directs BestMinds, a company specializing in awareness and intervention training for suicide and domestic violence. He has worked with cross-professional teams in counties with high suicide rates to develop prevention and intervention strategies; he helped shape the suicide prevention plan developed by the state of Ohio.

Russ has extensive experience in assisting organizations across the United States with strategic planning, mediation, customer surveys, and training. He has worked with many different kinds of organizations including churches, libraries, colleges, and an arboretum. He has developed training for organizations in strategic planning, conflict management, team building, staff morale, customer service, and enhancing board function.

As a former Presbyterian pastor, Russ served in small, midsize, and large churches in New York and Ohio. In that role, he was active in his regional association (presbytery) and worked in the areas of strategic planning, energy conservation, human sexuality, church consultation, presbytery staffing, and administrative oversight. He has served as a consultant to every level of the church in areas such as succession planning, strategic planning, and organizational assessment. He has developed congregational and regional association assessment tools and has maintained a substantial database on church characteristics and congregations of all sizes and contexts. He is the creator of Landscape®, an assessment instrument for regional associations, Pulse®, a staff climate assessment tool for larger churches and regional associations, and FocalPoints®, an assessment tool for boards and leadership teams.

He has developed a number of products for churches in transition. Russ coauthored a book with Carolyn Weese that was published in August 2004 entitled The Elephant in the Board Room: Developing a Pastoral Succession Plan for Your Church. The concepts of this book have been incorporated in a workbook developed to assist church leaders in pastoral succession planning. Using these materials, he has assisted some of the largest churches in the United States in developing succession plans. In 2008, he published The Fly in the Ointment: Why Denominations Aren't Helping Their Churches and How They Can. In 2012, he published Owl Sight: Evidence-Based Discernment and the Promise of Organizational Intelligence for Ministry, followed in 2015 by Transition Apparitions: Why Much of What we Know about Pastoral Transitions Is Wrong. Other works include Mountain of Light; The Story of Montana de Luz, published in April 2005; and A Second Day: A Hopeful Journey out of Suicidal Thinking, which was republished in April 2014.

Russ lives with his wife, Shawn, in Asheville, North Carolina. Together, they have six children and twelve grandchildren.

For further information contact:
J. Russell Crabtree
Crow's Feet Consulting
614-208-4090
russ@crowsfeetconsulting.com

Robyn Strain earned a Bachelor of Science degree, summa cum laude, in Math and Science Education at Cleveland State University. Her Master's work, also at Cleveland State University, focused on developing educational programs and techniques for teaching academically gifted students as well as advocating for their special needs.

Robyn began her work with churches over 20 years ago serving as the Program Director for a large multi-staff church. She left to raise her young family and has since worked in the private and public sector. She returned to work with churches and has been using organizational intelligence for over five years. As the Senior Consultant for Holy Cow! Consulting, her work has taken her from the East Coast to the West Coast to help leaders gain greater clarity about the health of their church.

Robyn and her son live in Nashville, TN. When she is not traveling, she enjoys gardening, training her dog Riley, and skydiving.

For further information contact:
Robyn Strain
Holy Cow! Consulting, LLC
888.546.4132
robyn@holycowconsulting.com